Project-Based Learning
with Young Children

Project-Based Learning with Young Children

Deborah Diffily
and
Charlotte Sassman

Foreword by Shelley Harwayne

HEINEMANN
Portsmouth, NH

Heinemann
A division of Reed Elsevier Inc.
361 Hanover Street
Portsmouth, NH 03801–3912
www.heinemann.com

Offices and agents throughout the world

Library of Congress Cataloging-in-Publication Data
Diffily, Deborah.
    Project-based learning with young children / Deborah Diffily, Charlotte Sassman.
       p.   cm.
    Includes bibliographical references (p. 169).
       ISBN 0-325-00447-1
    1. Project method in teaching. 2. Early childhood education. I. Sassman, Charlotte. II. Title.
    LB1139.35.P8 D55 2002
    371.3′6—dc21   2002002163

Editor: Danny Miller
Production: Elizabeth Valway
Cover design: Catherine Hawkes, Cat and Mouse
Cover and interior photos by Deborah Diffily & Charlotte Sassman
Typesetter: Publishers' Design and Production Services, Inc.
Manufacturing: Steve Bernier

Printed in the United States of America on acid-free paper
06 05 04 03 02 VP 1 2 3 4 5

Contents

To the young children in our classes
who make Applied Learning projects an intriguing venture for us.

Foreword

It was a clear, sunshiny early spring day in New York City when I sat on my back porch to read Deborah and Charlotte's manuscript for *Project-Based Learning with Young Children*. I recall thinking that the weather—crisp, clear, and exhilarating—was a perfect match for the contents of this important book. Through their sensible and practical approach to designing curriculum and teaching our youngest students, the authors give us pause to rethink the look, feel, and content of the classrooms we know best. They remind us that early childhood students can fully participate in the life of their classrooms, their schools, and their communities.

As I read each thoughtful chapter, chapters alive with the voices of real teachers and children involved in important real-world project work, I couldn't help but think of Marge Piercy's popular poem, "To Be of Use." The poet reminds us how human beings hunger for work that is real; in this book, the authors help us understand how the same is true of our youngest citizens. As they engage their students in real-world projects—everything from creating an informative museum-like Exhibit of Rocks and Fossils to a Plants in Containers project that decorates the side entrance to the school—Deborah and Charlotte help us to understand how project work supports their students' growth as readers, writers, mathematicians, scientists, historians, and artists.

Accessible informational texts, particularly guide books, how-to books, and technical manuals are often described as "user-friendly." Although this book is "reader-friendly" (filled with eloquently described essentials including setting up a classroom for project work; selecting appropriate projects and end products; creating project timelines; gathering resources; teaching skills through project work; providing models for end products; and monitoring, documenting, and assessing student work), the descriptor that really comes to mind is "student- and teacher-respectful."

It is so very apparent that Deborah and Charlotte treat their students and their colleagues with the utmost respect, awe, and admiration. They boldly and practically address such affective domain issues as creating community, guiding children's behavior, using respectful language, handling conflicts, promoting decision making, and developing interpersonal and communication skills. Throughout, they remind us to let children be children, inviting them to learn from authentic models in the real world, but not expecting them to be miniature adults.

Project-Based Learning with Young Children serves as a compliment to the teaching profession. The authors truly understand what it means to be the grown-up responsible for the lives of other people's children. They provide suggestions for handling the inevitable obstacles that educators face, including what to do when children lose interest, make bad decisions, or languish in a project that is going nowhere. Similarly, they deal honestly with such frustrations as the loss of administrative support, funding, or access to community resources. The authors also highlight the need for teachers to trust their own strengths as early childhood educators and to delight and take comfort in having professional company.

As a superintendent of schools, I eagerly await the impact this book will have on the early childhood classrooms I know best. No child will have to ask, "Why are we doing that?" No child will have to wonder why he or she has to work hard or do his or her best. No child will have to wonder what school learning has to do with life outside school. Then too, no teacher will have to consider how to reach a hard-to-reach student. No teacher will have to consider how to motivate, engage, or otherwise inspire students to take schoolwork seriously. Instead, for both students and teachers alike, school will have the potential to enrich, inform, and invigorate their lives outside of school, demonstrating that the reason we all need to be readers, writers, and problem solvers is to improve the quality of our lives at school, at home, and in our communities. In other words, both students and teachers will have discovered myriad ways to be of use.

Shelley Harwayne
Superintendent of District 2, New York City

Acknowledgments

Teachers who put children's stories into print must first of all recognize the children and their families. Without the wisdom of five-, six-, and seven-year-olds, this book could not have been written. Furthermore, we give full praise to our colleagues at Alice Carlson Applied Learning Center who daily mold and shape the concept of Applied Learning into rigorous, real-world experiences for children.

Those teachers who founded the school with us—Cindy Blevins, Jacquie Bridges-Sheppard, Dwight Cooley, Elizabeth Donaldson, Gracie Escovedo, Debbie Gerwick, Deborah Gist-Evans, Ric Grant, Kathey Ignacio, Jayne John, Cherrie Jones, Maria Lamb, Denise Menke, Linda Ramos, Jeannie Robinson, Yolanda Sanchez, Adrienne Taylor, Charles Williams, and Regina Woods—set a high standard for those who have followed. The countless after-school study groups, Saturday gatherings, and late-night phone conversations have strengthened our interpretation of how children best learn.

Elizabeth Donaldson began the journey of this book with us. We are appreciative of her organizational skills, writing contributions, and experience in Applied Learning projects. Thank you, Elizabeth.

We are also grateful to the people who responded to our initial draft. Joe Gonzales, Kathey Ignacio, and Beth Saladino gave us advice about how to improve the manuscript. And, we are grateful for the Sam Taylor Fellowship grants that helped fund research for this book.

Finally, we deeply appreciate our editor, Danny Miller. His work both strengthened and solidified our manuscript. Beyond teaching us about the writing/publication process, Danny made us feel comfortable as authors. He encouraged us when we needed it, criticized our writing when the manuscript needed it, and made us laugh when we needed that. Thank you, Danny.

Introduction

In 1992, Alice Carlson Applied Learning Center was opened as the only elementary school-of-choice in the Fort Worth Independent School District. That meant that children could apply to attend the center without a qualifying entrance exam; they need only reside within the boundaries of the Fort Worth ISD. Nineteen faculty members, some parents, and local administrators met in July 1992 to begin the task of creating a school to "challenge traditional assumptions about learning."

For two weeks the group worked together, shaping the philosophy, governance system, daily routine, and discipline plan for the center. We made small decisions, such as that each teacher could choose what he or she wanted to be called (by first or last name) and that children did not have to walk silently down the hall in lines. And, we focused on big decisions about how to implement Applied Learning in our kindergarten through fifth-grade classrooms.

For two years before Carlson was founded, approximately twenty teachers in Fort Worth met to define best practice and determine new ways to connect schoolwork to the real world. This group defined Applied Learning as a whole-class inquiry to answer what they called "an ill-defined problem." This meant that no one knew how the project might conclude. What these teachers did know is that in every Applied Learning project, students had to direct their own learning: defining the question to be researched, consulting many different types of resources, and producing a product that other people would care about.

The new Carlson teachers had this group's work as a foundation to define Applied Learning for elementary children. This was a comfortable basis for teachers working with upper elementary students. But no one in the group of twenty taught kindergarten, first, or second grade. The early childhood teachers were rethinking totally new ground. We struggled with questions about how to make Applied Learning appropriate for young children, how to teach five-year-olds who could not read conventionally to conduct research about a topic, and how to find a real audience for the work of kindergarten, first-, and second-grade children. That first year, it felt like we had many more questions than answers.

As we worked with our students and observed the ways children thought, the ways they approached project tasks, and the ways they learned, we became convinced that our implementation of Applied Learning was appropriate for young children and that they would receive multiple benefits from this approach.

While we are still occasionally asked to defend the use of Applied Learning with young children—asking them to make their own decisions about their learning, do research, examine adult models, use those models for their work, and share their learning with a specific audience—we have become more and more convinced that this approach to learning is extremely beneficial. Those who question the appropriateness of this model with young children come to understand it when they learn that the focus of a project's tasks is not perfection. Certainly kindergarten children do not attempt the kind of research that fourth graders do, nor do the work samples of kindergartners look like upper elementary students. We limited this book to the discussion of Applied Learning projects for kindergarten through second grade to help other early childhood educators understand how these projects are implemented with young children.

For those readers familiar with the National Center on Education and the Economy's (NCEE) definition of Applied Learning, you will find some differences. Near the time Carlson opened as an Applied Learning Center, NCEE began working with the Fort Worth Independent School District. Soon afterward, NCEE added Applied Learning to the areas for which they were developing "New Standards." Their 1997 publication, *Performance Standards: Volume 1 Elementary School* (NCEE), provided six examples of what they defined as Applied Learning projects. While these projects begin with an ill-defined problem, not all of them require the research and content learning found in our Applied Learning projects.

Finally, one note about the use of pronouns in this book. We struggled with the decision about how to present our projects and those of our colleagues. We decided to refer to all teachers in the third person, even ourselves.

Together, we have fourteen collective years of implementing Applied Learning projects with young children. We have witnessed dramatic growth in our students, and we credit the community of learners and Applied Learning projects for much of this progress.

As you begin to read about Applied Learning and think about implementing it in your classroom, keep the children foremost in your mind. We have observed dramatic growth in the children we have taught and could tell stories about each of them. One student came to Carlson as a kindergartner. Jacqueline clutched her mother's dress every morning for weeks. She was petrified of math and convinced that she could not learn to read. This shy child with no confidence in her own abilities grew both academically and socially beyond the expectations of her parents and teacher. A year and a half into Jacqueline's experiences with Applied Learning projects she was asked to speak about what it felt like to be adopted. She spoke with poise and confidence to a gathering of more 2,000 people. Working through many different projects, Jacqueline learned that she could answer hard questions, share what she knew, and make a difference in the lives of other people. Empowered children like Jacqueline are the reason for our belief in Applied Learning.

1

Early Childhood Projects:
An Introduction

Projecks can be edukashional. Projecks can be fun.
—TRAVIS

These are the words—and the first-draft spelling—in a letter Travis, a six-year-old, wrote to explain project-based learning. This book's purpose is the same, to help you understand the powerful learning associated with project work. It also contains support as you think about and begin implementing projects with young children.

There are many definitions of the terms *projects* and *project-based learning*. We write about projects based on our fourteen years of collective experience teaching five-, six-, and seven-year-old children using Applied Learning projects.

Definitions

Applied Learning is similar in many ways to other high-quality early childhood programs. You will recognize many good early childhood practices throughout the discussion of Applied Learning—constructivist theory, child-centered classrooms, class meetings to plan activities and solve problems. However, there are some differences you will notice when we describe the characteristics of Applied Learning projects.

Applied Learning

The term *Applied Learning* is essentially self-explanatory. Students apply what they learn while they are learning new knowledge or new skills. Beyond that, Applied

Learning teachers ensure that children relate the work of school to work outside the classroom. Knowledge and skills are always taught within a context that is meaningful to children.

Just as the learning is tied to the world outside the classroom, the atmosphere of Applied Learning classrooms is more collaborative than the "adult-in-charge" traditional classroom. Applied Learning teachers begin developing a community of learners from the first day of school. Everyone is considered to be both a teacher and a learner. Applied Learning classrooms are child directed. Teachers encourage even young children to make decisions about their classrooms and their work. These decisions range from simple ones about what color paper to use on bulletin boards to more difficult ones such as what they want to study for the first six weeks of school.

Authentic work, the sense of community, and children's decision making form the basis of Applied Learning, which, in turn, supports Applied Learning projects. This book focuses on projects within Applied Learning classrooms.

Applied Learning Projects

In *Applied Learning projects*, children select an area of interest and work collaboratively to research the topic. They are encouraged to locate and use as many different sources of information as possible. After completing their inquiry, they share what they have learned by creating a real-world product, examining models of the product, and planning for a specific audience.

During Applied Learning projects, students direct their own learning instead of merely following directives from the teacher. The content they study and the processes of learning they experience connect to the world outside the classroom rather than being prescribed by textbooks. Textbooks are not totally abandoned in project classrooms, but they serve as only one resource. Children consult Internet, print, and people resources throughout projects. Observation and "fieldwork" are also key sources of information when the topics lend themselves to these activities. Children learn academic skills as they need them to accomplish something that is a part of their work. Unlike most traditional learning experiences, projects are conducted over several days or several weeks, and each project ends with children sharing what they learned with a real audience outside their own classroom. In summary, Applied Learning projects are:

- Student directed
- Connected to the real world
- Research based
- Informed by multiple resources
- Embedded with knowledge and skills

- Conducted over time
- Concluded with an end product

Projects, in one form or another, have a long history in elementary schools' curriculum. Appendix A discusses the theoretical and historical foundation behind Applied Learning. Our experience has proved to us that the benefits of Applied Learning projects enrich and extend children's learning.

The following section relates Susan's story of a first-grade project. The way the children work with her, and with each other, illustrates how Applied Learning projects are carried out.

The Story of One Project

The students at Alice Carlson Applied Learning Center produce an Intercultural Festival every spring. Unlike traditional school carnivals that are planned and run by the PTA, at this school, children are in charge. Each class chooses a different country or culture, studies it, and plans a booth for the festival. Susan's class selected Mexico as their country to study.

To begin the study, Susan asked the children to create a KWL chart: "What We Know About Mexico," "What We Want to Learn About Mexico," and "What We've Learned About Mexico." They had done this before, so the children immediately began dictating "facts" that they knew about Mexico:

- They have mud houses.
- The people are poor.
- They eat tacos.
- There are dirt streets.
- It is hot there.

Several children disagreed with the "facts" being dictated. Rosa countered one fact with, "You don't know what you're saying. My grandma's house isn't a mud house." Much discussion ensued as children defended their statements. As Susan facilitated the discussion, she suggested that they change some of the conflicting "know" statements into questions for the "What We Want to Learn" heading. Then, as the children found out "for sure," they could write the answer to those questions under the "What We've Learned" heading. The class agreed.

As the project began Susan read aloud the collected books about Mexico. Children dictated sentences for their chart as they encountered statements that answered any questions or contradicted any of the "known" statements. They collected information in their individual research folders. Interest grew, and children began to bring artifacts to school that they had borrowed from family, neighbors, and friends: piñatas, woven blankets, pottery, and decorative ceramic tiles. Angelica brought Spanish newspapers and magazines. Two children downloaded information from the Internet at home, bringing in pictures and information about life in Mexico. Children brought their favorite Tejano CDs and some of their parents' tapes of traditional Mexican music to play in class.

Susan's students had more questions than they could answer through printed resources. "Could we interview someone from Mexico? Remember, we did that last time," suggested John. So Susan reviewed previously taught interviewing techniques, and the students developed a list of questions for interviews with three people who grew up in Mexico. Notes from these interviews were added to the research folders.

The interviews reinforced the children's fascination with piñatas. While everyone agreed that they would make a piñata booth, students were not comfortable with just planning an activity booth. Susan led a conversation with the children, commenting, "I'll bet you know more about Mexico than just about any other class in this whole school. How could you show the others what you've learned?" The children suggested several options for sharing their new knowledge: video, brochure, book, fact cards. Eventually the class decided to have the booth and also create informative posters to place around the school.

Breanna had recently visited a museum exhibit that had "Did You Know That . . ." posters scattered among the artifacts. She suggested using this format for the posters, and everyone agreed. The children decided that they should make posters on the following topics: geography, weather, where people live, clothes, and food. Everyone volunteered to serve on one of these committees except David. He wanted to make a poster about Cozumel and Cancun because he had visited both cities on vacation. Jimmy suggested a compromise, "We can be on these committees, and David can make his own poster. After all, he knows more about those places than we do." The class agreed with Jimmy's suggestion, and David worked on his own poster. Then, during project time for the next four days, children discussed which facts were the most important, whether they should revise until everything was spelled correctly, how to use their best handwriting, what colors they should use, who would write, and who would draw the borders and illustrations. Figure 1–1 is an example of one of these posters.

On the day of the Intercultural Festival, the first graders talked with visitors about their posters and sold chances to hit the piñata hung in the booth. As the children interacted with adults and children attending the festival, it was obvious that they had learned a lot of information, developed an assortment of skills, and felt great about their project and themselves.

All of the students learned important information and skills during the project, yet each child learned different things at different levels. Each child's research

Figure 1–1. Geography of Mexico Poster Created for Hallway Display

folder contained information. Some had only two or three sources; others had as many as fifteen different sources. The children wrote facts in their own words and asked Susan to photocopy pages from books and magazines. They wrote interview questions and recorded the answers to the questions after the interviews. They revised and edited their written work, and some typed their final drafts for the exhibit. All of these writing formats were completed at different levels. Still, all children researched questions about Mexico and worked together to create posters that helped others understand more about Mexico and the Hispanic culture there.

Characteristics of Applied Learning Projects

Throughout the project, Susan made sure that it followed the characteristics of Applied Learning: student directed, connected to the real world, research based, informed by multiple resources, embedded with knowledge and skills, conducted over time, and concluded with an end product. Each of these characteristics is discussed in the sections that follow.

Student Directed

In project-based classrooms, children are active learners. Susan's students decided what topic to investigate and how to research the topic. They decided what resources to use, how to organize what they learned, and how to present it to others. These general decisions were made by the group, and then, as individuals, each child became responsible for day-to-day decisions about what work he or she did.

Applied Learning teachers guide students through all parts of a project. On a regular basis, "children and teachers collaboratively evaluate what they did and why, what they will do next and how they will do it" (Trepanier-Street 1993, 26). Teachers think about questions that children might raise and are ready to guide them to available resources (Rankin 1998). However, this preplanning on the part of the teacher does not mean that she or he makes decisions about project details. Children still make the decisions. Through the teacher's reflection, he or she is prepared to lead children in making project decisions and to help children make connections between adults' work in the "real world" and the work children do in projects.

Connected to the Real World

Applied Learning projects are authentic. Using adult examples as models, children replicate the processes used by adults to acquire new knowledge. This ties the children's work to the work done by adults in the real world. Likewise, adult models offer examples about how to display information. Although young children cannot reach the sophistication of adult work, they can begin to develop the approaches that professionals use to conduct their work. When children choose a science-related project, they explore the topic in multiple ways like a biologist, a geologist, or other professional scientist. When children decide to create an informational brochure about what they have learned, brochures created by adults or older students serve as models. When children decide to write a book, they work through the stages of writing, from initial draft to peer response through revision and editing to a final published version, just like adult authors. In the case of the Posters About Mexico project, the first graders chose to create posters as comparable as possible to ones from a local museum's exhibit.

Because projects are related to the world of work and children continually examine how adults in various professions do their work, the children's learning takes on a different dimension. Young children's work doesn't have the sophistication of the adult model. Creating their work so it contains many of the characteristics of the model connects it to the real world. "Through projects, children understand that school learning can be applied outside the classroom" (Trepanier-Street 1993, 26).

Research Based

As previously mentioned, children are encouraged to approach their work in ways that professionals do—professionals such as authors, scientists, newspaper staff, etc. Research plays an important role. Whether the children are trying to find answers to their questions about a topic or creating an end product to demonstrate what they have learned, Applied Learning teachers encourage research—and explicitly teach children how to conduct that research.

Informed by Multiple Resources

In Applied Learning projects, children learn to consult many resources as they try to answer their questions. If they find a very informative book, they won't stop there, even if the book seems to cover the topic quite well. They continue looking for additional information. Teachers encourage children to find other books, talk to families and friends, search for appropriate Internet sites, and find people who are experts on the topic. Susan's students found information from all of these sources.

Whenever possible, research is also conducted "in the field" (Borgia 1996). The firsthand knowledge developed during a well-planned field trip cannot be replaced with any other learning experience. Children considering the possibility of planting and tending a flower garden visit a nursery, make drawings, ask questions of the employees, and take notes. Children who want to create a museum exhibit benefit from a field trip to a local museum where they focus on the details of one exhibit. Not every class can take a field trip for each project. Sometimes we plan a walking field trip to a nearby source of information or use the school environment for research on topics such as insects, birds, trees, plants, and so on. And when we return, the children always document their research, as shown in Figure 1–2.

From a First-Grade Teacher . . .

Children are just more actively involved when they work on projects. They care more. They remember more. Yesterday a child said to me, "Remember when we made those flowers for my mom and we cut those little stems off and had them grow in our class all winter?" That project was last year. They were really involved in watching their plants every day and recording the growth. They learned all kinds of science content from all sorts of resources during that project. That child wouldn't have said that if our study of plants was just learned from a book. He wouldn't say, "Remember when we drew that diagram of a plant?" That just wouldn't happen.

Embedded with Knowledge and Skills

Applied Learning teachers teach knowledge and skills when the students need them to accomplish something they are attempting within the project. As Lilian

Figure 1–2. Jorge and Christopher Documenting Their Research

Katz (1996, 20) states, "It's by using a skill that a child becomes really proficient. Good project work provides a real-life context for children to practice the skills they're learning." When this application of skills occurs, children remember the skills they have learned because they learned them in a context that was important to them (Trepanier-Street 1993).

Different types of skills are embedded in Applied Learning projects. This embedding offers children an opportunity to apply their learned skills; that is, go beyond memorization and skill practice to immediately applying what they learned to accomplish something important to them (Hartman and Eckerty 1995). Within projects, learning experiences are related, and these related experiences help children develop vocabulary, acquire scientific and mathematical ideas, and refine their literary skills. Perhaps the content areas of reading and writing are most easily included in projects. Whatever the topic, reading drives the research process and writing is used to document what is being learned. Depending on the topic of the project, knowledge and skills about mathematics and science can be embedded into the project, or the teacher may lead children into certain activities so that these skills are included.

During the Posters About Mexico project, Susan provided knowledge through the books, magazines, newspapers, and web pages that she read aloud. When the books in the classroom did not explain *los posados* as well as a student wanted, she found other resources for him, as she did often during this project. As children worked in small groups for research, Susan specifically taught short lessons on research strategies, writing the most important words rather than copying whole sentences out of a book, conventional spelling for words being used frequently, and other writing strategies.

From a Second-Grade Teacher . . .

As a project teacher, you don't have to "make" children learn. Within a project, they want to do it. They want to know how to do things. They want to have all the skills that they need to do the projects. You don't have to convince them that yes, they do need to learn how to plant seeds at the right depth and to learn that some seeds are planted deeper than others. They want to know that so they will be successful. You don't have to drill them on grammar and spelling. They want to know how to write clearly and to know how to spell words so that everyone can read their writing. They want to learn new things so that they will be successful.

Conducted over Time

Applied Learning projects are never short-term endeavors. They are conducted over a period of time as the children's interest continues. Most kindergarten to second-grade projects last from three to eight weeks. The main objective of a project is not to rush to the product, but to explore the process. Susan's class could have produced the same posters in two or three days. Susan could have shortened the project from three weeks to three days if she had decided the topic for each poster, assigned children to groups, and given each group the information they needed. However, this teacher-directed teaching approach would have limited the children's learning, if indeed any learning would have taken place as children copied sentences to create the posters.

From a First-Grade Teacher . . .
Now that I've spent a year doing projects with first-grade children, one thing strikes me as very important. It's the span of time we spend working on a connected endeavor. In the real world, there would never be a time in a company that anyone would spend thirty minutes focusing on marketing, then switch to accounting, discuss that for an hour, then switch again to the topic of sales for forty-five minutes. In schools, we chop up learning, spending a few minutes reading the social studies textbook, a few more minutes filling out a workbook page about a grammar rule, a few more minutes reading about science, again from a textbook. All of this ignores what children are interested in, what they want to know. Project work just makes more sense to me with children learning about a topic that interests them, learning skills they need to accomplish something they choose to do, and working on the same project over a period of time. All the learning is connected.

Concluded with an End Product

At the end of an Applied Learning project, children share with others what they have learned. This end product is more than just a culminating experience. This product is designed so that children share what they learned. There are many different ways to accomplish this: books, manuals, newspapers, brochures, videos, television scripts, museum exhibits, or position statements.

For every end product, children examine a competent model and define an audience for their work. Approximating the best, or most competent, model gives children a goal to work toward. Simply stated, the process of considering what information is most important and how that information could best be presented to others is more important than how the product looks. When researching Mexico, Susan's students decided to create posters similar to ones in a local museum exhibit. Of course, the first-graders' posters looked like first-graders' work. The lettering was not even; the drawings were not always representational; and facts were somewhat jumbled. The children's posters did not look like the slick, professional posters at the museum; however, they did the best they could approximating the adult model. As children continue to work on Applied Learning projects, the quality of the end product becomes more sophisticated. By the time children are in fourth or fifth grade, their end products look very much like the model they use. For young children—in kindergarten, first grade, and second grade—the process is always more important than the way the product looks.

Defining an audience for a product helps shape that product also. The first grader's posters were created with the needs of their audience (children who were interested in the Intercultural Festival) in mind. Deciding what the "other children would like to see" helped to shape the project's final product. The first-grade children knew that other children liked to see borders and illustrations so they included those things in their work. Children sometimes survey their audience to determine what is most appealing, much like field tests are conducted in adult work. Once again, as children become more sophisticated, their understanding of what appeals to an audience takes on clearer dimensions.

The Place of Projects in the Early Childhood Classroom

The story about Susan's first-grade students indicates that children develop considerable knowledge, skills, dispositions, and feelings as they work on projects (Katz and Chard 2000). However, as compelling as projects are, we do not believe that young children should spend the entire school day involved in project work. The students in our kindergarten and first-grade classes also engage in learning experiences that are characteristic of all good early childhood programs. We read quality children's literature and poetry to the class. Our students create paintings and sculptures, sing songs, and move to music. The children continue to care for class pets and plants and have daily opportunities to choose the learning centers in which they will work. And they play outdoors every day. We ensure that age-appropriate routines continue in our early childhood classrooms even when Applied Learning projects are implemented.

Project work does not replace regular content-related instruction. We teach reading in a variety of ways, such as shared or guided reading (Fountas and Pinnell 1996) or Drop Everything and Read (Bryan 1999). We engage in interactive writing (McCarrier, Pinnell, and Fountas 1999) and lead writing workshops (Oates 1997). We designate times for math (Parker and Richardson 1993), science (Saul et al. 1993), and social studies (Lindquist 1995; Manning, Manning, and Long 1997), although we do not feel pressure to engage all of our students in all of the content areas every day.

We don't mean to imply that projects are an add-on to our early childhood curriculum. Although we designate a block of time to work on projects—perhaps an hour a day—project-related work is often integrated throughout the day. Certainly, teachers should take advantage of children's interest in a project to carry over into other instructional times. For example, if a project requires measurement skills, we might plan mathematical instruction about measurement. If the project requires interviewing, we would plan a study of writing interview questions as part of writing workshop. We often use scientific observation logs to help children increase the detail they use in their drawing. This translates into more detailed drawings when the end product calls for drawings. We specifically plan integration of project work.

Comparisons with Other Approaches to Projects

In the world of elementary schools, educators use the term "projects" to describe a variety of experiences. Some teachers think that any activity continuing for more than one day is a project. Reading a book and producing something other than a book report is called a project. Creating a papier-mâché mask or shaping a sculpture is referred to as an art project. An experiment carried out for a school's science fair is regarded as a science project.

Some educators differentiate projects from other educational experiences more precisely. Using the term "the Project Approach," Lilian Katz and Sylvia Chard (2000) define a project as "an in-depth study of a particular topic" (2) and describe projects as experiences that "should extend over a period of days or weeks, depending on the children's ages and the nature of the topic" (3). In his book *Starting from Scratch*, Steven Levy (1996) describes a year-long project, What Is the Ideal Classroom?, as his "most complete attempt in setting high expectations, giving students responsibility for their own learning, and involving the community in the schools" (xvi). In other chapters, he describes projects in which students research the origin of their town's name and determine the biggest change in their town in the past decade. In discussing his project-based classrooms in the book *A Democratic Classroom*, Steven Wolk (1998) discusses meaningful and purposeful learning as students participate in actually doing things, not just reading about them. Each of these approaches (see Appendix B) to projects is sound, and all approaches have some characteristics in common with Applied Learning projects.

Benefits of Applied Learning Projects

As we implement Applied Learning projects with young children, we have observed fairly profound growth that we attribute to project-based learning. From our observations, we believe that children remember and use skills learned through the process of researching a topic and creating an end product more often than in traditional education. We also believe that children learn social skills not typically learned in elementary schools. And, possibly, the most important impact we observe is the way children come to view themselves as they work on projects.

Remembering and Using Skills

During projects, children learn skills as they need them to accomplish a specific task. They learn how to write a business letter when they need to write a letter to someone outside their classroom. They learn to use an index when they are researching a specific topic within a project. Children remember skills they use and apply them in subsequent situations.

It is not just skills that children remember over time. They also remember the knowledge they gain during their work on a project. Because they choose the topic of projects, the topic has personal meaning. They pose questions and find answers on their own. They record this knowledge and consider ways to share their learning. Because of the high level of personal involvement, children remember what they have learned as they work on projects.

From a Kindergarten Teacher . . .

I arrived early for a parents' meeting at my son's middle school when I heard my name shouted across the auditorium. It was one of my former students who was now in high school. We hugged, just like in kindergarten, and I asked how things were going for him. He told me school was okay, then, in a much more excited voice said, "I'll bet you didn't know that I got a part-time job at the museum. They let me work in the science lab. I'm cataloging fossils. That's because of you. Remember when we did that project in kindergarten? We learned all about ammonites and worm tubes and pancake clams, and we could tell people what they were, and most adults that came to our museum didn't even know what a worm tube was." Robert went on to talk about that exhibit and how it connected to the paleontology work he was doing now. I was impressed. Robert was recalling facts about fossils that he learned eight years ago.

Social Skills

Project work requires interpersonal skills not typically expected of young children. By working in groups, children learn how to back up their own opinions with reasons and how to compromise when they don't agree about how to proceed with the project. They learn conflict resolution techniques to solve problems among themselves or to reach decisions that need to be made. These are rather sophisticated skills, but through teacher modeling, role-playing, and repeated experiences, young children develop these skills as part of the process of projects.

During Applied Learning projects, students learn to interview "experts" to find answers to their questions, and they always ask for feedback about the end product they are creating. So, while they work on projects, children learn more about interacting appropriately with peers, children in other classes, and adults outside the school.

Feelings of Empowerment

After two or three projects, young children come to think they can find answers to any of their questions from books, people, or their own observations. They see themselves as knowledgeable in many ways, but always more knowledgeable about their project's topic than the audience for whom they create the end product. Because "other people" are going to see their end product, their work takes on a more significant dimension in the minds of the children. Our students refer to their project work as "important work."

Challenges to Implementing Applied Learning Projects

Travis's words at the beginning of this chapter—"Projecks can be edukashional. Projecks can be fun."—are true. So is the last sentence Travis wrote in his explanation of projects—"Sum tims projecks cn blo up in yr face." Perhaps Travis overstated the reality of project work, but solving problems is an integral part of the process.

The Posters About Mexico project, as described earlier in the chapter, sounded as if it went very smoothly; however, like any project, there were some problems that had to be solved. Some children wanted to research Japan because that is where their favorite cartoons were made. Children argued over the color of posterboard that they should use. One of the committees "threw together" their poster, and it was less than acceptable by the class's established standards. There are problems in every project, but solving problems is an integral part of the learning. Some of the problems that can be anticipated are discussed in the following sections.

Children Can Make "Bad" Decisions

In responding to young children's decision making, it is important to remember just how young they are. They are just beginning to learn how to contemplate choices and state reasons for their preferences. We support children as they are learning these skills, even if they appear to us to be "bad" decisions. Sometimes a decision makes perfect sense to five-, six- or seven-year-olds, and adults just can't understand it. We have to decide if a decision is one we should try to reverse, or if it really doesn't matter from an educational perspective.

A decision that did need to be changed came at the end of the Rocks and Fossils Exhibit project. As that project drew to a close, the children developed an interest in the rain forest. After one child shared an article about the Costa Rican Children's Rain Forest, the class agreed to donate one hundred dollars to preserve an acre of it. They were confident that they could earn the money by selling their rocks and fossils to adults and children at the school. So the kindergartners decided to dismantle their exhibit and start selling the rocks and fossils on the next Monday.

Meanwhile, the executive director of a local charitable foundation heard about the Rocks and Fossils Exhibit and called to arrange a tour. But he could not come until the following week, and the class had already decided to start their sale. In an effort to accommodate this influential friend of the school district, Deborah explained that "an important man wanted to come see their museum" and asked the children to "keep the exhibit open for a few more days." The children voted twenty-two to zero to stay with their original plan. She tried again, explaining the situation in more detail. The second vote was twenty-one to one. Deborah asked the children to think about this problem over lunch.

She knew that demanding that the children reverse their decision would undermine all that the children were learning. Deborah called another class meeting after lunch and explained *compromise*. She asked the children to "think very seriously to see if anyone can come up with a solution where everybody gets what they want." After a few minutes of discussion, Julia quietly shared, "Why don't we get half the rocks and fossils and start our sale, then Mr. Williams can see the museum with only half of the rocks. And we should put a sign on the door that says, 'If you had come on time, you could have seen all the rocks and fossils.' " Deborah's use of the pondering strategy paid off—the influential visitor and administrators were appeased and the children still made the decision.

Another decision made within that project had a different outcome. When the kindergarten children decided to create a museum exhibit after they studied rocks and fossils, they visited a science museum. They talked with the museum exhibit staff about issues like signage. Despite what they saw at the museum and what they heard about creating exhibits, the children decided that, in their exhibit, they would have orange posterboard with purple lettering. This was a first project for this class and Deborah was concerned about how parents, all new to concept of Applied Learning, would respond to a kindergarten-created exhibit. Despite her concern about the orange and purple signs, the truth was it really did not matter what colors were used for the signs. It was the children's exhibit, and they should make the decisions.

From a Kindergarten Teacher . . .
I remember going in to eat lunch after a morning of project work. My nerves were frazzled! Thankfully, my colleagues had been through the same thing and were sympathetic. When I started projects, I never thought I'd spend all morning mediating decisions about how a display's border should look or how many books you should consult before saying the research was finished. I have to remember that the children are learning more through these discussions than they did when I simply decided for them and told them what to do. But it does try my patience!

Children Lose Interest

Occasionally young children will decide to pursue a particular project, but as the days pass, their interest diminishes. If the interest level begins to drop, we often encourage the children to continue for a few more days. Sometimes we say, "It seems to me that you guys are not as interested in this project as you were last week. Can we talk about how you are feeling about your research?" It may turn out that the children just need some additional assistance in finding resources. Or it may be that the children thought they would be interested in the topic, but they really are not. It is important to let children know that they can change their plans or even stop work on a project, but not at the "drop of a hat." This decision is taken seriously and children are encouraged to support the decision to end a project. Before children make this decision, we often lead a discussion about alternatives.

In the case of Charlotte's Insect Exhibit project, students began a project with the idea of creating a museum exhibit. They had just finished creating another exhibit, and they loved the attention they got from acting as museum docents and giving tours of their exhibit. So, overwhelmingly, they wanted to create another museum exhibit. The children selected the topic of insects and seemed interested in their research. They found dozens of books about all kinds of insects and brought in field guides to identify the insects they were collecting. They watched a video about insects and downloaded information from the Internet. Charlotte planned a Saturday morning family field trip where the children and their parents met at an open field to collect insects. The research phase progressed as expected, but something didn't feel right as the children began to create the end product. The children were not displaying the same level of enthusiasm as they had during the creation of their first exhibit. Charlotte brought up the subject during a class meeting and several children expressed frustration they were feeling—"the insects are too hard to catch," "they're too small to make a whole museum from them," and "it's too hard."

Charlotte might have cajoled the children into staying with their original plan, but did not see an educational reason to do this. Instead, she commented, "Could we have a different product? Could we, say, make a calendar?" That was enough to redirect the conversation. Over the next three days, the children examined calendars, chose twelve insects to feature, sketched those insects, and drafted short paragraphs about each insect. In this case of children losing interest, the teacher decided to redirect the children's interest into a different end product. Charlotte could just as easily led the children into a decision to end the project. There is no decision that is best. As Applied Learning teachers, we try to consider all factors of an issue and make the decision that seems best at the time.

The Project Is Not Going Anywhere

Occasionally, the class reaches a point where they are revisiting the same resources, drawing the same pictures, and recording the same facts. Obviously, something is wrong. We cannot allow children to languish in this state of repeated activity that has no continued educational purpose.

In Deborah's class, following a week-long author study of Tomie dePaola, the children continued to be fascinated with dePaola's books. During a class meeting, Mike announced, "You know what? I bet we know more about Tomie dePaola's books than anybody in the whole school." Deborah decided to build on this comment and see if an Applied Learning project might emerge. She explained that people who knew "a lot" about books sometimes shared that knowledge through book reviews. Over the next two days, she shared examples of book reviews from the children's section of the newspaper, journals that publish reviews of children's books, and several catalogs of children's literature. Julia commented in class meeting, "I think we should make a catalog, just of Tomie dePaola's books, and we could put it in the library, and other classes can read our catalog if they want to find a Tomie dePaola book that they will like." Deborah was so proud of her students. With only a nudge from her, they had come up with the topic and an end product for a project.

Two weeks after the decision to make a catalog, the children were still drafting and drawing. None of Deborah's musings, ponderings, or think-alouds could get the children to begin discussing how to get from their individual work to a class-created catalog. Every time she broached the subject, the children responded with comments to the effect of needing to draw more pictures first. Rather than letting the children continue, Deborah decided to take a fairly directive "wondering aloud" approach:

> I just thought of something, so listen very carefully and see if you can agree. I wonder if this would help us . . .

17

After lunch, let's put all the Tomie dePaola books in the middle of our circle. Then you find a partner and make sure that you two can be serious workers together. Select three or four books that you both would like to review. Take those books, paper, and a pencil with you to a quiet place in the room, and we will spend all afternoon writing, revising, and editing those reviews. Will that idea work for us?

Three days later, the entire catalog was finished, copied, and bound.

When the project seemed to stall, Deborah made the decision to guide the project to its next stage. If the children had still been learning, she would not have stepped in. However, the children were caught in a cycle of repeating the same task. So she made the decision to push the children into a decision to conclude the project. Sometimes a teacher's direct actions can move the project along, but, at other times, things beyond her control affect a project's outcome.

Outside Influences Affect the Project Negatively

At times, the project stalls, and it has nothing to do with the students or the teacher. There may be problematic outside influences that cannot be rectified. Sometimes necessary permissions are withdrawn. Sometimes the experts who have been identified do not understand the concept of student-directed projects and do not cooperate. At other times, the children make a decision that will require more funding than the teacher has access to. Teachers have to make decisions about how to talk with the children about these problems.

ADMINISTRATORS CHANGE THEIR MINDS   Administrators sometimes have trouble understanding and supporting project work. Principals have to approve many parts of project work, such as field trips for firsthand research, the purchase of resources for research, the use of space within the school to display information, and so on. Sometimes a decision is made, and the class proceeds on their work based on the principal's decision. Then, for reasons not totally explained, the principal reverses a decision and the project comes to an abrupt halt.

Carlos's second-grade students were researching guinea pigs, planning to write a "how to care for guinea pigs" manual. Two students had located Jimmy Harris, a man who bred guinea pigs, and exchanged several emails with him. When the boys shared the emails with the class, everyone agreed that they needed to go on a field trip to Harris's house. A committee was formed to write a proposal to the principal for permission. With permission granted, another committee organized the field trip: coordinating with Mr. Harris, asking parents to drive, making sure that parents' insurance cards were copied and on file in the office, and deciding how lunch would be handled. The students were excited about seeing all kinds of guinea pigs and having many of their questions answered. The day before the field trip, the principal sent a note to the class that she had received a memo from "downtown" saying that parents were no longer allowed to drive on field trips. The children were devastated. They brainstormed solutions to the problem, but no district buses could be scheduled for the next day. Mr. Harris was leaving town the next week and would be gone for more than two weeks. They had already made publicity posters announcing the how-to manual would be available on a certain date—two days before Mr. Harris would be back in town. One administrative decision changed the focus of this project.

EXPERTS WILL NOT TALK TO THE CHILDREN Project teachers lead their students to believe that they can talk to virtually anyone and get their questions answered. We want children to feel empowered to seek out information from any source they can think of.

One afternoon, as Deborah's first-grade students were working on a Reptile Exhibit project, Robert asked if he could borrow her cell phone to find out the name of a lizard. She agreed and helped him look up the phone number of two pet stores. Robert dialed the first number, listened, and asked his question. He was puzzled when the person at the pet store hung up without answering. He tried the other store with the same results. Robert sighed, and said, "I'll call Ken. He'll talk to me." Moments later, Deborah heard him leave the following message:

> Hi, Ken. This is Robert from Deborah's class. My committee is the Snakes and Lizards committee. Today we are working on lizards that we know about, and we can't think of that lizard you showed us that changes colors. We need to know. I am calling on Deborah's cell phone but we can't leave it on, so will you call the office and just tell Joyce and she will write us a pink note. Thank you, Ken.

Ken, the education director at the local zoo, had met these children when they were on a field trip two weeks before. He knew how seriously they were taking their research. Within minutes, Ken called Joyce, the school secretary, and left the message: "It is a chameleon." When a child from another class brought Joyce's note to the class, none of the students were surprised. There was no question in their minds about Ken returning Robert's call. They believed that anyone they called would return their calls, but this is not always true.

After experiences where adults think the children are only "playing on the phone," we contact the adult expert before the children make their phone calls. We try to ensure a successful experience for both the children and the person they call. While this is an easy step to overlook as you become accustomed to the children's competence, it is important to the children's success. "Experts" don't mean to be rude to students. Some just do not expect serious phone calls from young children.

THERE IS NO FUNDING FOR PROJECTS   Teachers also have to deal with the issue of money. Very few projects can be implemented without some level of financial investment. Even when the resources for research are borrowed from families, friends of the class, public libraries, or other community organizations, materials may have to be purchased to document and organize information and/or create the final product. In some schools, funds are not available for even ordinary supplies such as posterboard, index cards, and pocket folders. Supplying these would not require a large expenditure, but the funds have to come from some source.

Numerous schools have a set-aside fund available to teachers who need materials beyond typical classroom use. These funds can be requested by a teacher, but Applied Learning teachers would most likely turn this into another part of the project. We would suggest that the children write a proposal explaining what they need to buy, why they need the materials, and how much money would be required.

If funds are not available at the building level, project teachers have few options. Teachers who have developed close relationships with students' families often ask them to purchase some of the materials needed for the project. And, as in most elementary classes, many Applied Learning teachers buy supplies for the class.

There are definitely problems associated with Applied Learning projects. However, we view these problems as continued learning experiences—for the children and for ourselves. And, when we consider the challenges in light of the benefits of projects, we are convinced that Applied Learning projects will always be part of our work with young children.

Summary

Applied Learning projects offer a powerful learning experience for young children. Because project-based learning is child directed and connected to the world outside the classroom, these students learn much more than the specific content included in a project. They realize that they can find answers to their questions and that multiple resources are available. Children develop skills that are needed to accomplish their work. When they stay with one topic for an extended period of time, children learn to plan and implement their plans. And, perhaps most importantly, they learn that they can explain what they have learned to other people. The experiences involved in Applied Learning projects empower children to learn and share their learning.

2

The Applied Learning Classroom

Creating an atmosphere that encourages students to interact, feel independent, and take pride in the upkeep of their classroom is crucial for everything we do throughout the year.

—Joanne Hindley 1996

Long before the first day of school, we spend hours considering how we will arrange the classroom. We know that the room's arrangement encourages and supports the types of work that will take place in that classroom that year. An Applied Learning classroom is a place where children do their work, just as a studio is structured to support an artist's creative endeavors or a law office meets an attorney's needs. We try to anticipate the needs of our new students and arrange the room to meet those needs.

Our schedule looks much the same as any child-centered early childhood classroom. While our role as teachers is often the same as any good early childhood teacher, there are some differences in the way we listen and respond to children while teaching them to solve their own problems.

Organizing the Room

Much of the work of young children takes place in learning centers. We arrange these centers to support children's work. The children are encouraged to talk as they work, so noisier learning centers—blocks, art, dramatic play, sand, and water—are grouped together, as are quieter ones—reading, writing, listening, and math. Special areas in the room are created to support whole and small groups. We organize materials so that they are easily accessed. And, we try to create an aesthetically pleasing and supportive environment.

The Room Itself

The way our classrooms are arranged, the centers available to children, and the materials provided in each center are critical to the teaching and learning that goes on. Experienced educators create a physical environment that conveys the message that "this is a place where (children) will be safe, comfortable, and where they will do interesting things" (Bickart, Jablon, and Dodge 1999, 99). While there is no single right way to arrange and organize the classroom, we offer some suggestions that work for us in our Applied Learning classrooms.

As the room's arrangement is planned, areas are fashioned for whole-group, small-group, and individual activities. While each of these areas has unique needs, the spaces blend together to form the whole classroom.

AN AREA FOR WHOLE-GROUP ACTIVITIES   Our classrooms have a sufficiently large area where all children can gather together comfortably. We often define this area with a large rug or set it off by couches. We sit as a whole group, with an easel nearby, easily accessible to everyone. This holds chart tablets and markers we use in group planning. Our class meetings are held here, and plans for project work begin here. It is a place for discussion, reflection, and study. Figure 2–1 shows Charlotte leading a class meeting in such an area.

From a Second-Grade Teacher . . .

Having taught for many years in a classroom where the children sat in desks arranged in straight rows, I was amazed at the difference when the children gathered on the carpet for group activities. The ways we talked were different. In rows, the children didn't face each other and most of their interaction was with me. Our carpeted area allows us to look at each other, and there is much more discussion and interaction. The circle puts us all on an equal footing, and now I find that many times the children lead the discussion.

SPACES FOR SMALL-GROUP ACTIVITIES   While shared activities and discussions often occur in large groups, much of young children's work and learning occurs in small groups. Our arrangement of the room provides spaces for small groups to work.

During project work, students often work together in "committees" (a more real-world name for small groups). During the Posters About Mexico project, described in Chapter 1, the first-grade students worked in committees as they prepared their posters. Two groups elected to work on the floor. One chose to kneel at the low table, while the other one gathered around the Lego® table with clipboards. We don't bring in extra tables and chairs for committee work. We try to

Figure 2–1. Charlotte Leading a Class Meeting

provide sufficient storage in each learning center so tables in centers can be cleared and used for committee work. Other permanent small-group areas in our classrooms have included raised carpeted platforms, lofts, or low cabinets that children can use as counters.

SPACES FOR INDIVIDUAL ACTIVITIES Young children do not choose to work with other children at every moment of the school day. Just as our physical environment supports large- and small-group activities, it also provides small cozy areas in the classroom for private spaces. A child may prefer to write while sitting in a small space between the wall and a filing cabinet. Another child may choose to sit on a pillow in the corner and create a "wall" with hollow blocks so he can read privately. Still another child may choose to work in the listening center, listening to quiet music while she works. Offering children these choices extends the idea of a child-centered learning environment and helps them learn to make appropriate decisions.

Obviously, no two Applied Learning classrooms look the same. Teachers create their own environments and personalize the classroom using some touches of home. Art prints hang beside children's paintings. Plants are placed strategically around the room. Attractive baskets hold collections of books. A small table with a soft-light lamp positioned between two bean bag chairs gives the reading center the feeling of reading at home. To soften the classroom, some teachers add upholstered furniture, tablecloths, curtains, silk or dried flower arrangements, fabric-covered walls, and quilted wall hangings.

In order to furnish our classrooms, we have become creative in soliciting donations as well as in finding bargains. We tell our families what we'd like to have in an ongoing "wish list." Our local secondhand store holds a sale on couches and other upholstered furniture every other month. Parents shop garage sales and have sewn new covered cushions for shabby couches. We have stopped at the curb on trash day to pick up something that someone was throwing out. These items may not last but a year or so, but if the price is low enough, we get good wear from the items.

Materials

Children learn best when they are encouraged to explore and investigate. Active learning is supported when materials are logically organized, labeled, and within the reach of the children. "If the materials in the classroom are well organized, attractively displayed, and labeled, children know where to look for information and locate materials to help them investigate and represent their learning" (Bickart, Jablon, and Dodge 1999, 106). We provide sufficient quantities of materials, making them readily available so our children have choices and can easily accomplish their work.

Applied Learning teachers always consider the skills they want children to develop during the school year and think of ways to model those skills. Storing and labeling materials, books, and community supplies demonstrates a variety of organizational techniques that children can emulate.

From a First-Grade Teacher . . .
Until recently, I kept all the materials in cabinets and only brought out things as the children needed them. I think I was concerned about losing materials or having to sort them after the children were finished. Another teacher suggested that I involve the children in the organization and labeling process. She pointed out that I may be sending a negative message about the children being a part of a community and being valued by putting myself in charge of supplies. After taking her advice, I was pleasantly surprised to see the children making choices and accepting responsibility for putting the materials away.

Organization of materials in an Applied Learning classroom is essential as the children work on projects. They need frequent access to books, magazines, paper, writing tools, art supplies, and manipulatives that enable them to measure, weigh, count, and compare. A child who spends a great deal of time looking for the book on rabbits for his research, the date stamp for her notes, the stencil of the letter *N* for a poster, or a tape measure to determine how big a shark is in relation to the bookcases in the room, delays the progress of the project. As shown in Figure 2–2, we pay particular attention to the kinds of storage containers available and which ones, or combination of ones, best suit the needs of the children. Labeling logically organized materials adds to the accessibility. We provide a variety of manipulatives and books that are interesting and engaging to children as they work on projects. We also gather supplies for writing and art in a central location for the use of all students. The organization of the manipulatives, books, and community supplies enables the children to work independently and make the best use of their time.

We involve our students in the arrangement of the room and the organization of supplies. We value their opinions, and they are usually right on target. For example, Charlotte's first graders, who had worked together during their kindergarten year, kept the felt-tip markers, crayons, and pencils in baskets on each table. In their class meeting, they decided to "let anyone get anything they needed from any basket—without having to return it to a certain table." They de-

Figure 2–2. Example of Organized Learning Materials

cided that returning the markers to the right basket just "made some people argue and want to keep all the markers." Their strategies were successful—the supplies were shared by the whole class and fewer skirmishes occurred over the markers. This seemingly small decision made a large impact in the classroom. Charlotte allowed, even encouraged, the children to make a decision about the room's arrangement that affected them. They were learning to be responsible for their own actions.

BOOKS AND OTHER PRINTED MATERIALS   An abundance of books and other print material is essential in Applied Learning classrooms. They are one of the basic resources for project research and must be organized so that they are easily accessible by the children. "However different the classroom libraries look and operate, all teachers demonstrate that books are revered and must be treated with respect" (Harwayne 2000, 18).

While it is almost impossible to have too many books, it is necessary to make them appealing to the children. Baskets or plastic containers placed on low bookshelves allow children to see the front and back covers of books, instead of only the spines. Books that have some commonality can be grouped together. For example, we often place books written or illustrated by the same person in one container, with the appropriate identifying label on the container. We also group books and label them by author, category, or genre. For example, categories such as the following could be used:

- ABC books
- Atlases
- Counting books
- Dictionaries
- Fairy tales
- Nursery Rhymes
- Magazines, newspapers, or catalogs
- Poetry books
- Science books
- Social studies books
- Song books

The organizational method used in the classroom must make sense to the children who need to locate books. We begin the school year with a few books grouped into two or three categories. As the weeks pass, we bring more and more books into the classroom. The children are a part of the decision-making process about how books are arranged. Having an active role in these decisions helps the children remember where different books are located and helps build a sense that "we are all in this together."

SUPPLIES   Just as sharing decision making builds a sense of the class as one entity, sharing supplies also contributes to the feeling of the class as a group. We make supplies available to the whole community by arranging supplies on each table, in each center, and/or in easily accessed areas of the room.

We gather some supplies in cups, cans, small baskets, or trays, such as:

- Standard pencils, colored pencils
- Colored markers, crayons
- Paper, brushes, paint
- Erasers, pencil grips
- Stapler, staple remover
- Scissors, glue, tape, hole punch

Additional materials may be found with our community supplies or may be stored in the writing or art centers:

- A date stamp and a stamp pad
- Paper—white, manila, construction, newsprint, etc.—in a variety of sizes
- Lined paper—teacher-made or commercially produced
- Posterboard or cardstock
- Story paper with area for pictures
- A folder/file system for storing finished and unfinished work
- Thread, yarn, needles, paper fasteners, etc. for bookbinding

Learning to negotiate the use of community supplies is a skill that serves children well as they begin project work. During all phases of a project, children negotiate sharing resources and materials. Something as simple as introducing community supplies at the beginning of school starts building the skills needed to implement projects successfully.

From a First-Grade Teacher . . .

I was used to having little pouches tied to the side of each child's desk to hold their individual supplies. But when I decided to group the children together at tables, there was no place for the pouches. So I got some little plastic baskets and put all the supplies on the table—a set of markers, a box of crayons, and enough pencils for each child at that table to have three pencils. At first I wanted the children to keep the markers and crayons in the box, but I quickly realized that was a waste of time. Now I just pour them into the basket and the children can access the materials as they need them. I store the extra crayons, markers, and pencils in a cabinet so children can replenish the baskets as needed. This system works and helps the children develop that sense of responsibility to the other people at their table. The other supplies, like glue and scissors, are stored in community baskets on a bookshelf. I even started putting scratch pads and self-stick notes in those baskets.

From a First-Grade Teacher . . .

When I started using a process approach to teaching, the most challenging thing for me was putting the supplies out for the kids to use anytime they wanted. I thought I was the adult in the room and I knew what the kids needed. I wanted the stapler, the tape dispenser, the staple remover, and the magnetic holder for paper clips on my desk. I eased myself into the change by purchasing duplicate supplies for the children and keeping separate ones for myself. That's embarrassing for me to admit now because the supplies are all over the room and I like being able to get a stapler if I am over by the writing center or grabbing a piece of scratch paper from the home center. Sharing the supplies is a good thing now for the kids and for me.

LABELING   Just as in a well-organized office setting, classroom materials are organized so that children can get the materials they need easily. We label virtually all storage containers to help children locate and use materials independently. Sometimes we type or print the labels ourselves so that each label is the same size and spelled conventionally. Then these words become models for the children to recognize and use in their writing. Other times we choose to have the children make the labels. In either case, the children see a functional purpose for print (Teale 1995) and are applying a real-world skill.

From a Kindergarten Teacher . . .

Prior to the beginning of the school year, I printed labels and added an illustration for the areas in the room—*library, writing center, science center, math center, art, blocks, listening,* and *dramatic play.* Early in the school year, as the children began to look for materials, they quickly realized—with some "pondering" from me—that the room needed more organization. After much discussion, the children sorted the containers of manipulatives into two categories—math and science. Then they made labels, using the ones I had made earlier as models. I was thinking of the language arts and math skills that this activity taught but I also found that the children were proud of their accomplishment and felt ownership in the classroom. Finding materials was not a problem after this. Later in the year, the children organized and labeled all of the books in our classroom library.

Schedule

We believe that young children learn more effectively when they feel secure in the classroom. One of the ways we provide this security is through a predictable daily schedule. There is nothing sacred about the schedule we use. However, these learning experiences, in this order, have worked for us.

Arrival
Class meeting
Read-aloud
Writing/reading workshops
Self-selected centers
Poetry reading
Lunch
Math menu
Recess
Self-selected centers
Class meeting
Read-aloud
Dismissal

You'll note that time for projects is not built into this schedule. That is because at the beginning of the school year, children are not yet involved in project work. For the first few weeks of school, we concentrate on building a sense of community (Chapter 3) and introducing pre-project experiences (Chapter 4). When we do introduce projects, we schedule about an hour in the afternoon for project work, rearranging the afternoon schedule.

Of course, there is a lot of flexibility in our daily schedules. We do the same things in the same order every day to support the children's sense of security, but the length of time devoted to each activity varies from day to day. If our students are especially engaged in math activities, we extend math menu and spend less time that day working on projects. On the other hand, as we near the conclusion of a project, we may spend an entire day or two on a project. You may decide to start smaller and devote thirty minutes a day to project-based learning. The decision about how much time to devote to projects and when to schedule project work is clearly the teacher's prerogative.

The Teacher's Role

As we said in Chapter 1, the relationship between the teacher and students during project work is that of mentor and apprentices. Most teacher roles are the same as they are in child-centered classrooms. Teachers prepare the environment and plan learning experiences that meet the wide range of needs found in most early childhood classrooms. However, as we help children answer their own questions and solve their own problems, we realize that some of these roles are especially important to the success of student-directed projects. To accomplish this, we actively listen to children, responding to their requests and statements, and use the strategies of reflecting, pondering, and wondering to guide children as they make decisions about their learning.

Reflecting, Pondering, and Wondering

Listening carefully to children is important if you are going to help them answer questions and solve problems. We often repeat back to a child what he or she said, but in our own words. Taking the children's remarks seriously validates them as learners and instills a sense of confidence and pride that no other experience can inspire. Teachers are used to giving children direct answers to questions; however, Applied Learning teachers use the techniques of reflecting, pondering, and wondering as they guide individual and class discussions.

While it seems that we are recommending that you take a "backseat" role in discussions with your students, it is important to remember that, in reality, this role is far from "backseat." Our role is to pose questions and nudge the discussion along.

REFLECTING In group discussions, we find it effective to provide neutral responses—"That's one idea. Who has a different one?" We make other comments that encourage children to express all of their ideas and thoughts—"Could you say more about that?" or "Do you have anything to add?" We respond to an individual child's comments by restating what he or she said to us. We might also use these phrases:

- "Wow!"
- "Really?"
- "I don't quite get it. Can you tell me again?"
- "Well, now what?"
- "I'm amazed!"

Reflecting back to children is helpful when listening to their ideas. Often children just need to hear their ideas expressed aloud. Speaking thoughts aloud clarifies and organizes them. During the Posters About Mexico project described in Chapter 1, Antonio was struggling with his decision about what border to put on his poster. He said, "I can't decide if I should draw suns or put raindrops on my border because Mexico has a lot of sunny days but it rains a lot in the mountains too." His teacher, Susan, responded, "Hmmm . . . , suns and raindrops." "Suns and raindrops?" repeated Antonio, "That's it! I'll make an ABAB pattern of suns and raindrops." It is the quiet, reflective response that is often most effective in guiding a child to think for him- or herself.

PONDERING Pondering is a way of modeling deeper thinking about a question. Young children don't readily look for deeper meaning, clarification, or nuances.

We resist the temptation to directly answer or solve a child's problem. Statements such as these are helpful to us:

- "I'm not sure. Who could we ask?"
- "Hmmm, really?"
- "Now that sounds interesting."
- "Hmmm, what do YOU think you could do?"
- "I wonder where we could find that?"
- "What are our options?"
- "How could we do that?"
- "If that IS happening, what could you do to make the situation better?"

When children are "stuck" on a question or idea, pondering can guide the learning. Elizabeth's class had just started a project to research and write a manual about what animals make the best class pets. At recess, a couple of boys ran up to her and announced that they thought a cheetah would be a good class pet. Her first instinct was to say, "No, we can't have a wild animal in our classroom." This statement would have ended the conversation. Instead of stating what she thought was the obvious, she stopped and pondered, "Hmmm . . . , a cheetah, do they make good pets?" The boys both responded, "Yeah!" before they ran back to find their friends.

Later, the boys brought up their idea during a class meeting. The boys had an answer for every concern voiced by Elizabeth and other children:

"We only have a small cage—My dad can build a bigger one."
"A cheetah is a meat eater—We can get the leftover food from the cafeteria."
"A cheetah is dangerous to have in our classroom—We'll get a gentle one."

At Elizabeth's suggestion, the boys spent a couple of days researching cheetahs. For every new fact about the wild animal, the boys came up with a counter statement that would make it acceptable to keep a cheetah as a pet. Only when these boys contacted a mammal expert from the local zoo and got the information that "a cheetah is an endangered animal" did they reluctantly agree to remove cheetah from the list of desirable pets because "if every class got one, then there wouldn't be any more cheetahs in the whole world." If Elizabeth had said the first thing that came to mind during recess, the boys would not have learned about a topic that interested them. Memories of making a sound decision about what makes a good pet would not exist. One pondering question opened the door for the boys' learning both about cheetahs and about how to solve problems.

Of course, the boys and Elizabeth knew from the beginning that a cheetah could not be a class pet. But because the teacher acknowledged the possibilities of their suggestion, rather than dismissing it immediately as impossible, the boys had the opportunity to learn a valuable lesson about supporting their beliefs with facts and thinking through possible alternatives.

The technique of "pondering" puts the responsibility for learning back to the children. If a teacher says, "When we went to the zoo, one of the staff answered our questions. Write a letter to him and ask your questions," the idea would be a direct command from the teacher, written only because the teacher said so. This "top-down" method of facilitation is not appropriate in Applied Learning projects because children don't play a part in the decision. Instead of making an announcement to students about writing a letter to zoo staff, we would approach the issue in a different way. We would probably inquire, "Where do you think we could find answers to your new questions?" or "Is there anyone we know who might be able to answer these questions?" If no child in the discussion thought of the expert at the zoo, we would continue to pose questions, to lead the children into an answer. In projects, the teacher is still teaching—but the impetus is coming from the children. As Steven Levy (1996) states, "Herein lies the art of teaching; leading the students from their own experiences to the depth and breadth of the world" (29).

WONDERING   At the beginning of a Bat Display project in Charlotte's first-grade class, she listened, with a puzzled look on her face, while the children argued over a basic concept. Jennifer, Justin, and Kelton defended their convictions about bats being birds. The other children in the class were positive that bats were not birds and argued that they were right. She knew she needed to intervene to stop the argument. Charlotte could have said, "Okay, now, bats are not birds. Let's move on in our discussion." Instead of giving the answer, she responded to the class, "If you think bats are birds and you think they are not birds, I wonder who is right? How can we find out for sure? Can we find out more information?" Thus, by wondering aloud, she led the children to discover the answers for themselves.

Other statements that help us with wondering are:

- "Some people want to _____. Others want to _____. How can we decide what to do?"
- "It seems to me that _____. Do you think we might _____?"
- "I saw fifth graders who had a problem like this. They _____. Could we try that?"
- "Doesn't your aunt know about _____? I wonder if she could help us?"

This reflecting, pondering, and wondering extends to all aspects of children's classroom work. Responsibility is put back to the children to solve interpersonal conflicts, keep up with materials, take care of themselves, and make important decisions about project work. "That's a decision you need to make" is an oft-used phrase in our classrooms.

The Children's Role

Just as our role during projects is different from the role of teachers we remember as children, our students also assume different roles. We expect quite a bit from our students, but we explicitly teach the behaviors necessary for project work, and we support children as they assume these roles.

During Applied Learning projects, children direct their own learning, making decisions as a class and individually. The entire class decides which topics they study and how they go about the process of learning about those topics. As a group, they decide how to share their learning with others. Daily, each child decides what he or she will accomplish during project time. This role of decision maker is new to most children entering a project-based classroom. They don't automatically make good decisions, but learn decision making over time.

Children who work on projects undertake the role of group member in a variety of different groups. In order to be an effective group member, children learn many different interpersonal skills: stating what they want from another person, talking to peers respectfully, negotiating differences of opinion, setting goals for the group, and implementing plans made by the group.

We also expect children to assume the role of a "serious worker," a term coined by our students. "Serious workers" do the work they have agreed to do, are self-controlled, and work both independently and in groups. We also want each child to be a "creative thinker," asking the "what if" questions, thinking "outside the box," and suggesting better ways to accomplish a task. While these may seem to be rather sophisticated roles for young children, with our continuing support, they learn to assume these roles over time.

Summary

The physical arrangement of the room, the organization of the supplies, and the displays are carefully considered in an Applied Learning classroom. Children need to explore, experiment, and wonder within a secure and rich environment. Therefore, the teacher provides working space for whole-group, small-group, partnered, and individual activities. The wide variety of materials in the classroom are organized in such a way that children can gather supplies and find resources independently. Both teachers and students assume active roles that may be different from their previous experiences.

3

Creating a Classroom Community

A community is a place where individuals share common values, goals, and activities. It is a place where each member takes on roles to provide sufficient services so that the community's goals are reached. In communities, everyone does not do the same thing at the same time, but groups work together to achieve common goals. A community is a place where social bonds are established and individuals can flourish.

—Sue Bredekamp and Teresa Rosegrant 1992

Most of us face a new group of students every year. They walk into our classrooms on the first day of school as virtual strangers. Our priority, along with academic achievement, is to help the children become responsible, self-reliant learners. We do this by building a sense of community where children make cooperative decisions and work together in collaboration and partnership. Before beginning the first Applied Learning project in your classroom, it is critically important to establish this sense of community—and to provide a range of pre-project experiences, discussed in Chapter 4.

We take purposeful steps toward creating a community of learners from the very first day of school. We begin to establish respectful relationships, orally modeling with I-statements, such as, "I noticed that you came to the group area for our meeting." Children follow our lead in the language and tone of voice we use with them, such as, "Thank you for returning your marker to the basket. That makes it easier for other children to use it too."

Classrooms as Communities to Support Project Work

During the first few weeks of school, we concentrate on creating a sense of community. We begin to develop this community by embedding the needed skills into our curriculum blocks—modeling desired behaviors, establishing routines to support those behaviors, and looking for strengths or interests in each child.

Modeling takes place throughout the day. We model respectful ways to respond to a request—"I appreciate you letting me know we are out of paper in the writing center. There is more on the back shelf if you'd like to get it." We highlight children's respectful responses—"Thank you, Cherrie. I noticed how politely you asked Sylvia for that marker."

We establish routines to support the desired behaviors, such as listening when one person speaks—"When you are speaking, how does it feel when everyone looks at you? Do you want everyone's eyes on you when you talk to the group? Okay, let's turn our bodies so our faces look at the speaker." During our shared reading, our initial lessons focus as much on listening as they do on responding to a book. In early math and science experiences, we focus as much on group dynamics as we do on learning content. In this context, the way children interact with each other is as important as the academic knowledge and skills that they are expected to learn.

These shared experiences help children begin thinking of themselves as a group. We also sing songs or recite poems together, with these becoming "our" class's poem or song. For example, we read (and reread) Jack Prelutsky's poem *The New Kid on the Block*. Each time we read that poem, we act astonished about the "bad" things that the new kid does and someone always comments that no one in our class would ever behave that way.

We know that "each child has strengths or interests that contribute to the overall functioning of the group" (Bredekamp and Copple 1997, 16), so we begin looking for those qualities. As Jimmy shows an interest in the science center, we name him the "science center expert" and refer other children's questions about the science center to him. When Renee announces that her birthday is next week, she becomes responsible for locating books about birthdays to share. In everything we do, we reinforce the idea that this class has come together for important reasons—playing, learning, and caring for each other (Wolk 1998). And, because we know that we will be implementing Applied Learning projects in the weeks to come, we take this sense of community further, introducing the concepts of decision making, responsibility, and communication.

Characteristics of a Community to Support Project Work
Decision Making:
- Making and carrying out decisions relating to their work
- Sharing in the decision-making process

- Reaching consensus about group decisions
- Supporting their decisions with reasons

Responsibility:
- Cooperating, trusting each other and the teacher
- Depending on each other for help
- Accessing and returning necessary materials and supplies

Communication:
- Understanding the give-and-take of conversation, talking and listening
- Expressing genuine concern for their peers, making friends, sharing, and speaking to others respectfully

Decision-Making Strategies

As we help young children learn to make their own decisions, we teach them a variety of strategies to use. They may only know to "argue until they get their way." It is our job to introduce different aspects of decisions—voting, individual decisions, and group decisions.

> **From a Kindergarten Teacher . . .**
>
> "That's a decision you need to make," comes out of my mouth several times a day. Young children are accustomed to having adults direct their behaviors, even about simple stuff that the children could manage themselves. Often a child will ask, "Can I put my sweater in my locker? I'm hot now." And I respond, "That's a decision you have to make." Our class's agreement is that sweaters go on the body or in the locker. Some children are in the habit of waiting for an adult to say, "Put that in your locker." They don't think for themselves.

From the beginning of school, children are involved in making decisions, sometimes as a group and sometimes as individuals. In Applied Learning classrooms, children quickly learn many ways to make group and individual decisions. Different strategies work best at different times and in different situations.

VOTING   Voting is one decision-making strategy that is introduced on the first day of school. This allows the teacher to quickly establish that decisions in the class will be made by the group, and to introduce the most basic decision-making method, voting. In Marta's kindergarten class, she introduces the concept of "choice," then offers two books for the class's read-aloud. Both books meet the educational goals set for that day so either book is okay with her. She shows the books to the class and introduces a simple thumbs up, thumbs down way of voting

Figure 3–1. Children Voting "Thumbs-Up, Thumbs Down"

for the book to be read (see Figure 3–1). Then she reads that book to the class, re-marking that she will read the other one later in the day.

Learning to make group decisions by voting can be difficult for some young children. Those who are accustomed to making their own decisions at home have difficulty accepting that their choice may not be selected by the group. These children may act out, pout, or otherwise be uncooperative. Voting on an unemotional issue, such as which book to read first, is an effective strategy that helps children adjust to this type of group decision making. When the children realize that both books will be read and that the vote is simply to decide which one will be read first, it is easier to accept votes that don't go their way. This, in turn, helps to lead the group further along the continuum toward consensus as a decision-making method.

GROUP DECISIONS Learning to make group decisions is important because many decisions that guide a project are made in small groups. Likewise, knowing how to participate as groups make decisions is a lifelong skill. An adult who participates easily in the give-and-take of decision making has an advantage over the person who has not learned this skill.

Not only do we encourage each child to make decisions, we also specifically plan decision-making experiences for children in groups of two or three, as well as

37

at the whole-class level. For example, when Jorge gets out paint for his kindergarten class's art center, he asks two children for help in deciding which colors to offer that day. The two children discuss the colors and come to a decision, telling Jorge which colors to put in the art center. Likewise, he asks three or four children to listen to an audiotape of action songs and choose the next one to teach the class. On hot days, Jorge might present the option of having recess early in the day when it is cooler or at the accustomed afternoon time. In each of these situations, the children are introduced to consensus—a much more sophisticated style of group decision making. Note that teaching consensus is easier managed in a small group where each child has an opportunity to share his point of view.

INDIVIDUAL DECISIONS   Another way we introduce decision making in a classroom setting is to allow children to choose their materials. For example, as we observe the children during Writers' Workshop, we reinforce the concept of individual decision making by commenting on their choice of writing tool—"Oh, you decided to use a pencil instead of a marker. So that's better for you?" By offering choices and reinforcing that they made an appropriate decision, we are taking the first steps toward establishing that, in this class, children make decisions about many facets of their learning.

We believe children need to be comfortable in making decisions. Some of the children's first decisions in our classrooms will be choosing which center to work in and which center materials to work with. This choice can occasionally be overwhelming for some children. If they have been in a previous group setting where they were directed, they may not know how to look at all the centers and make a choice. In this case, we narrow the available choices. We suggest two centers and allow children to choose from them. This generally increases the comfort level of the child enough to enable them to make informed choices.

From a Kindergarten Teacher . . .
When a child can't decide on a center, I help him along. I often ask, "Are you in a building mood? Do you want to make something?" If the reply is yes, I point out the block center, the Legos®, and the Polydrons®. The child can then focus on those and pick one. If the answer is no, then I suggest centers like puzzles or Play-Doh®. Just asking about what they want to do helps them define which center to pick. Of course, teaching children to make choices takes much more time than it would if I directed, "Go to wooden blocks today." I've come to realize that these little snippets of time that I spend with individual children help each child to become better at making decisions. So even though it does take more time, it is worth it, because as they become more comfortable, they become more independent.

While we believe that children need to make decisions about their work, we also believe that the choices children make should be within parameters we set. Bobbi Fisher (1998) confirmed our thoughts about children's decision making well when she wrote, "I have decided that the children should read every day—a managerial choice. I plan time for reading and supply reading materials—books, magazines, newspapers—from many genres of fiction and nonfiction. Within this framework, the children choose what and where they will read, whether they will read alone or with a friend, when they will read" (11). When we make these kinds of general decisions for the class, we provide the boundaries the children need to make appropriate choices.

Responsibility

Developing children's sense of responsibility is important to us. In our project-based classrooms, children's responsibility extends to decisions they make about what to learn and how they carry out their research. Children are responsible for the final product, working responsibly with others to accomplish their goal. Before children can begin to be responsible, they need to feel competent. We find that many young children have developed a sense of learned helplessness. They don't always view themselves as capable of making their own decisions or taking care of themselves. Often they have been taught to look to adults, first their parents and then their teacher, to tell them what to do. Our mission is to instill in children a confidence in their abilities and in the abilities of their peers. Project work can be difficult if children are hesitant to act independently, and we make every effort to instill feelings of competence and interdependence in our students. We accomplish this through creating experts in our classes, directing children to other children, and teaching communication strategies.

CREATING EXPERTS   Children feel competent when they are successful at what they do. In Applied Learning classrooms, children come to depend on each other for answers and help. This is not something that happens automatically. It is something we orchestrate as we build our community. We have found it particularly helpful to identify, in every child, a strength that can be publicly announced as an area of expertise.

One thing we do is hand routine tasks over to our students. For example, in Charlotte's kindergarten classroom, she realized that tying shoelaces somehow became her job (and one she didn't like). She considered her options. She could either continue to tie shoes, or she could use this situation as a springboard to build interdependence and positive peer modeling in her class. Charlotte noticed that Sarah and Dontell were particularly adept at tying shoes, and she asked them if they would like to be the class's "experts" in tying shoes. The children were happy and she was free from shoe tying. Moreover, Sarah and Dontell were given the chance to shine in front of their peers.

Other children become class "experts" because of some knowledge they bring to the class or a specific skill they know or learn. A child who has had pet hamsters for several months can be presented to the class as the expert on how to pick up the hamster without chasing it around the cage for several minutes. Another child can become the listening center expert. At least half the time when the listening center is not working, it is because the pause button has been hit accidentally. In a matter of minutes, we can teach a child to recognize this problem and fix it. With some close observation and several "training" sessions for individual children, we find ourselves doing fewer routine classroom tasks and our students taking more responsibility for these things. It may be hard to find an "expert" position for every child in your class, but we think it is worth the time invested. The children who are asked for help from their peers feel valued and important. Over time, these feelings develop into feelings of competence.

DIRECTING CHILDREN TO OTHER CHILDREN   Beyond referring children to class experts, we search for ways to get children to ask each other for help. This helps the children to relate as peers and to see each other as resources in the class on many levels. Here are some examples:

- "Cynthia, I know you can't hear when it's a C or a K. Kate has been working on words that start with C. Check with her or see if Joyce has the word "cookie" in her writing dictionary."
- "If you want to write the date on your journal entry, perhaps you could ask Carlos to help you count down on the calendar to find today's date."
- "Hmmm . . . , I wonder if Amy could help remember how to play that math game. She was playing it yesterday, I think."
- "You need the stapler? Check with Sarah. I think she was using it a minute ago."
- "I'm not sure. Who have you already talked to?"

When we direct children to other children, we are modeling language they could use to ask for help or for information. Learning appropriate ways to talk with each other is an important part of building a community of learners and a necessity for successful project work.

Communication Strategies

As early childhood teachers, we recognize that talking to each other is fundamental to young children's learning, as they learn best by talking and doing in a social context (Fisher 1998). As children verbalize what they are doing and question each other, they are extending their learning.

We do not expect young children to come to school understanding the complexity of the give-and-take of group discussions. We teach appropriate behaviors for talking and listening in group situations, model these behaviors, and create situations for children to rehearse the behaviors. We teach children behaviors such as:

- Listening to one person at a time
- Looking at the speaker
- Restating the speaker's position for clarification—"Regina, did you mean to say . . . ?"
- Building on what was last said—"What you said reminds me of . . ."

Adults use a variety of strategies when they communicate. While young children may come to school ready to talk, they don't always possess a repertoire of communication strategies. So we teach children to look at the speaker, ask for clarification when needed, or check for understanding by restating what was said. Additionally, we teach children to make connections with what was said, personalizing the information.

For example, at the beginning of the year, we might lead a group discussion about what it looks like when a person is being a good listener. A simple brainstorming session occurs, and we record the children's ideas on a large chart. We select one of the more concrete behaviors, model it through role-playing, and practice it as we listen to each other.

From a First-Grade Teacher . . .

I use chart tablets to record what goes on during our group discussions. That way we have a record of the discussion—even if it is in my sometimes messy printing. I tell the children that I am not using my best writing because I'm trying to get the ideas down—just like they do in their first-draft writing. I can flip back through the pages to find a rubric or list that we have previously made. The need for those lists keeps popping up all through the year. If they are on chart paper, you don't have to keep recreating the list, just add to it.

These kinds of conversations about "the way we do things in our class" continue throughout the year. We present an issue to the children, involve them in the discussion, clarify a point or two, and then involve the children in putting the agreed upon behavior into practice. These conversations help clarify social expectations and can be used to reach group consensus about classroom issues.

From a First-Grade Teacher . . .

It is December and the room parents are anxious to plan the winter party for the children. This particular year, they tell me that they want to bring a plain cake, let the children decorate it, then serve it with punch to drink. I remind them that it is really the children's party and they make their own decisions. During a class meeting, I brought up the parents' suggestion. Instead, the children wanted cubes of cheese, raw carrots, chips, pretzels, and Ranch-style dip followed by "fancy, decorated cookies." Three volunteers wrote a letter explaining the class decision and sent copies home with all the families. The children declared it the best party ever! They learned about ways to get what they wanted. The room parents were impressed with the children's planning and happy to help implement that plan.

As we plan lessons for the children, we build in situations for the children to practice these communication strategies. For example, the important part of the learning sometimes takes place after the task is complete—in the class's review of what was done. In Joy's first-grade class, she brings the children back together to review what they learned about a particular topic. She leads the discussion, asking each group to explain how they shared the work, tell how it went, and describe any problems or successes. As the children make their reports, she begins a list of "Good (and Bad) Things to Do When Working in a Group," as in Figure 3–2. This

Figure 3–2. Example of Teacher Transcribing Children's Comments

list evolves for a few days with items being added or changed. Over time, it becomes the basis for the class's rubric for group work. Joy is creating a situation in which children must communicate with each other, and she is teaching them how to communicate most effectively.

Shared Experiences

As teachers, we strive to develop the feeling that "we are all in this together" over the first few weeks of school. We specifically plan learning experiences and activities that involve everyone in the class, in order to directly support the sense of community among the children (Kohn 1996).

Classroom Routines

Predictable schedules create a routine that the children learn and come to expect. For example, in Wesley's class, children know that they will choose their own learning center after the morning read-aloud and that lunch comes right after they share poems. In Sarah's class, the children use a pocket chart to set the routine for the day. Sarah arranges sentence strips labeled *reading, writing, math, lunch, center time*, etc., in the order they will occur for that day. The children refer to this chart, reinforcing that there is a daily schedule.

Within the daily routine, the academic subjects also follow a predictable pattern. Writers' Workshop always begins with a minilesson by the teacher, then each child states what they hope to accomplish for that day. Independent writing follows with the teacher circulating through the room, holding conferences with individuals and small groups. The time period culminates as the children publicly share their work in the "Author's Chair." Even within this routine, children follow response group and "Author's Chair" procedures. Likewise, math instruction begins as the children gather in the large-group area for a shared lesson. After the teacher's presentation, they divide into smaller groups to play games that reinforce the learned skill. Other procedural routines include how the children access their lockers, sharpen their pencils, or get books to read.

Shared Rituals

Rituals also contribute to the children's greater sense of community. Sometimes rituals simply emerge from the life of the class. Kevin plays soft music as his students arrive each morning. He wants to establish the feeling that this classroom is a relaxing place to be and different from the hall or the room next door. The class enjoyed the music he was playing and began to bring tapes and CDs to share. As a group, they decided to play soft music at writing time and to play loud music during clean-up time. Playing different kinds of music for different activities became a ritual for Kevin's class.

Just as this ritual emerged, others can be planned. As Becky thought about rituals and the morning lunch count, she decided to change the way the children did the count. One morning she whispered to the class, "Today we are going to do something special. Let's get very quiet." Becky turned out the lights and retrieved a flashlight from a nearby cabinet. She then whispered, "If you are getting your lunch on a tray today, stand up very, very slowly." Silently, twelve children rose to their feet. She pointed the flashlight at the child nearest to her and whispered, "One," and indicated that child should sit down. Moving the light to the next child, she whispered, "Two," continuing until all the children were counted and had sat down again. She continued asking children to stand for: white milk, chocolate milk, baked potato, or salad, the other cafeteria choices. The lunch count ritual was established—from that morning on the lunch count was taken in the dark with a flashlight. Over time, the children took over the role of holding the flashlight and filling out the lunch count form.

We believe that rituals are important in the process of building a community of learners. We also value the way teachers and children go about accomplishing their work (Denton and Kriete 2000). It is not a matter of finding the "right way" to conduct Writers' Workshop, prepare for afternoon dismissal, or choose a center in which to work. We consider the physical arrangement of our classrooms, observe our students, and strive to create routines that make sense for the children and ourselves. A group of children sharing routines and rituals becomes a community of learners over time.

Guiding Children's Behavior

The teacher's response to a child's behavior makes a difference in that classroom. The teacher who asks rather than tells, suggests rather than demands, or persuades rather than controls avoids power struggles while encouraging children to be self-regulating (DeVries and Zan 1994). This idea of self-regulation, or self-control, is integral to successful project work, as well as essential to success in life. We spend a great deal of time helping children understand self-control, but believe the time invested is worth it in the long run. One way we guide children's behavior is through discussions during class meetings.

Class Meetings

Class meetings are an important part of guiding children's behavior. Essentially, class meetings are times to talk—a forum for students and teacher to gather as a class to reflect, discuss issues, or make decisions about the ways they want their class to be. Our role is to create an environment in which children's learning, opinions, and concerns are taken seriously. The students' role in these meetings is to participate as valuable and valued contributors to the classroom community (Developmental Studies Center 1996).

During the first few formal class meetings, we work to establish respectful guidelines. We lead conversations about how to treat each other, engaging the children in discussion, and translating it into guidelines such as:

- We let one person speak at a time.
- We listen to each other.
- We can disagree with each other.
- We respect other people's opinions.
- We tell the facts of the problem.

From this starting point, we have regular class meetings, at least one every day. Some days the class has several meetings, ranging from a twenty- or thirty-minute planning meeting to a five-minute problem-solving meeting. Often a planning meeting is held in the morning to outline the day's work, several problem-solving meetings are interspersed during the day as needs arise, and an end-of-day evaluation meeting wraps up the day's activities.

Class meetings take different forms as the needs of the class change. At the beginning of the school year, many meetings focus on agreement about class norms or behaviors expected from the children and the teacher. Appropriate and inappropriate behaviors are discussed frequently. One day we might select the block center and discuss what self-control would look like in that center, or talk about behavior that would be appropriate in the cafeteria.

We always practice behaviors that are agreed on in a class meeting. We use specific examples of what the rules mean. The children role-play, pretending to have a problem. For example, when getting the children's attention was a problem for Linda, the class decided that she could "clap in a pattern" when she wanted the class's attention. So all the children spread out across the room, pretending to be writing. Linda walked around the room, pretending to hold brief conferences. Then she quietly said, "Oh, I need to tell everyone this," and then she "clapped in a pattern." The children practiced zooming their eyes to her, each trying to be the first to stop what they were doing to look at her. In other situations, practicing with puppets or flannel board figures can help young children understand the rules they are setting.

Designing Rubrics for Behavior

As the school year begins, we work collaboratively with the children to create simple rubrics that define desired behaviors. Issues are introduced during class meetings—"We have to walk from our room to the cafeteria. How will we organize our-selves to do that?" Children's background knowledge of "how to walk in the hall" often elicits answers ranging from, "Walk directly behind the person in front of you with your hands clasped behind your back" to "Make a line" to "Just walk there." As we lead the discussion, children might offer additional solutions—ask other classes how they walk in the hall, observe other classes as they walk in the hall, ask the principal what he or she thinks is good hall behavior, and so on. If they don't, we use the strategies of pondering, reflecting, and wondering aloud to elicit them. As these options are explored, children identify qualities of good "hall walking." Not-ing these and contrasting them with undesirable qualities begins the structure for a rubric. The qualities are listed in a "Yes/No" (happy face/sad face) format. We re-visit this rubric as often as is needed, depending on the behavior.

The evaluation of desired qualities and rubric making extends to other facets of the school day. Other behaviors—in the cafeteria, on the playground, and in the rest room—can be defined, while desired behavior for group or individual work can also be outlined.

Self Control

Self-control involves two aspects of behavior—how children conduct themselves during the day and how they respond to another person or idea. Young children tend to respond impulsively. They don't evaluate possible responses or think through consequences. Emphasizing self-control puts the responsibility for choos-ing a response with the child.

We establish what "being in self-control" means while brainstorming ways to act in a self-controlled manner. For example, during a class meeting about "push-ing," we would list children's suggestions about "what to do when you are pushed." We want them to see alternatives to retaliating impulsively. Children role-play sit-uations in which self-control is important. Reminders to "use self-control" and in-dividual discussions are ongoing. We believe that anything we can to do to instill a sense of responsibility for behavior is beneficial to the children.

From a Second-Grade Teacher . . .

I was walking down the hall to go to the office and here comes this small child run-ning straight toward me. As he neared me, I knelt down so I would be at eye level with him. I put my hand on his shoulder and in my most serious voice, I said, "Ex-cuse me, are you in self-control?" He looked down at the floor, then back up to me, and responded, "No, I'm in kindy-garten." It was so hard not to laugh. I reminded him that our school had a rule that everyone had to walk inside the school building. That incident reinforced for me how important it is to help young children learn ex-actly what we mean by the words we use.

Respectful Language

In order to respond to conflicts appropriately, children must learn respectful language. We begin by teaching the children simple I-statements to use to express their feelings. For example, when one child bothers another child, the latter child says something to the effect, "I don't like it when you _____." This kind of I-statement clearly defines the behavior that the child does not like and lets the first child know exactly what is annoying. A child might inadvertently bother another child and this simple statement clarifies any misconceptions. The first child's response acknowledges the second child's statement. Often children reply, "Okay, I won't do it anymore," or "I didn't know you didn't like that." Apologies are usually not called for, but the misunderstanding is cleared up in a respectful way. When children have not used words to solve problems, the language may be foreign to them. Other effective I-statements include, "When you _____ I feel _____" or "I feel _____ when you _____."

Talk-It-Over

"Time out" where children are sent away from the group for breaking a rule can be punitive and humiliating. But offering time to "talk-it-over" is encouraging and empowering. This is another strategy we use in resolving conflicts. We often designate two chairs in the room as the "talk-it-over" chairs. After a conflict, the two children sit in the chairs and face each other while working out a compromise. For the first couple of months, we sit beside the children and suggest specific language they might say to each other or ask questions to lead the conversation. When David accused Tara of pushing him, Charlotte knelt beside the talk-it-over chairs and listened for a moment. It was clear that the children needed support to work out their problem. Charlotte said, "Tara, David says you pushed him. Did you mean to do that?" When Tara shook her head, Charlotte said, "Then maybe you need to tell him that it was an accident." Tara did not respond, so Charlotte repeated her question. Then Tara looked at David and used Charlotte's words. We teach the skills necessary to carry out this procedure, helping the children practice listening to another person's side of the story, telling his or her side, and arriving at a compromise. We lead class discussions and the children role-play how to "talk-it-over." We follow up by facilitating conversations between children. This occurs frequently at the beginning of the year, but we have found that within a few weeks, most children are talking-it-over without our help. Figure 3–3 shows Terri helping three of her students to solve a problem.

Bringing the Disruptive or Reluctant Child into the Community

The misdirected behavior of some children constantly interrupts the work of the class. As well, children who avoid work on a regular basis present a challenge. We deal with these situations in a straightforward manner.

Figure 3–3. Terri Supporting Children Trying to Solve a Problem

We begin by looking for the underlying reasons for the misbehavior, tailoring our response to best meet the child's needs (Nelsen and Glenn 1996). For example, if a child seems to be seeking undue attention or acting out, she might be seeking approval or only feel important when noticed. Then we tailor our response to this underlying reason for the misbehavior, perhaps recognizing the child's accomplishments in front of the class, giving that child a special greeting every morning, or asking that child to take on a special responsibility in the class. By responding in a proactive way, we head off possible disruptions.

Because of the interactive nature of projects, the misbehaving child can be even more disruptive than normal. Referring to the class-created rubric for behavior during project time helps to focus the misbehaving child's attention. It often includes behaviors related to voice level, appropriate responses, being a serious worker, etc.

We use a predictable series of steps to deal with misbehavior. An initial warning about or redirection of the behavior sometimes solves the problem. If subsequent misbehavior occurs, we talk privately with that child to explain that perhaps he or she needs some help with her (or his) self-control. We ask that child to look around the room and choose a place where he or she can be self-controlled. We help that child articulate appropriate behaviors for that area of the room, with words such as, "Okay, you've selected the listening center. Can you tell me what I will see when you are in self-control there?" If the behavior continues to be inappropriate, we typically say, "It seems to me that you really do need help with your self-control, so I am going to choose where you will work until _____ (lunch, shared reading time, etc.)." This third step gives us the flexibility to help meet that particular child's needs. Some children calm down when they are running their hands through sand, so asking them to work in the sand center makes sense for those children. Other children are calmed by listening to soft music, sitting alone in a private place (reading a book or drawing pictures). And, some children need to be close to us, so that our physical presence and/or quiet reminders support the child's emerging self-control. If a child is truly out of control, we might even suggest that he or she work in another classroom. We would have discussed this with the other teacher ahead of time and identified a student in that class to work with our student.

The child who avoids work or consistently repeats the same incorrect answer presents another challenge. Sometimes we pull these children into smaller, more focused groups where our teaching is tailored to reteach needed skills. These children often feel inadequate. They avoid work that they do not believe that they can do. Small-group work allows us to target those skills a child needs to practice. Because the same academic skills are repeated in project work, we constantly support those children who need extra help.

Some days, a child simply is reluctant to work with friends. When that occurs, we apply the same kind of "help with self-control" approach. At the third reminder, we might ask that child to work alone or near us. Whatever the decision we make about disruptive or reluctant children's behavior, we try to ensure that our actions do not embarrass or humiliate them.

Summary

Establishing with the children a respectful community of learners based on decision making, responsibility, and communication begins on day one. Classroom "experts" are developed and celebrated. Children depend on each other and collaborate. Through shared experiences, we teach, model respect and responsibility, and foster children's social and academic achievement. Group decisions are made during class meetings as children learn compromise and mutual concession. Conflicts are solved by the people involved using resolution techniques, including collaboration, respect, and listening. All young children benefit from learning these types of behaviors; however, this sense of community and responsibility is especially important for Applied Learning projects.

4

Before the First Project

Learning how to work productively in a group is a skill worth learning. It is of lifelong use. Consider the time spent on this not as taking away from (your teaching) but as a part of your plan of teaching. Learning how to do anything requires doing it, thinking about it, discussing it, revising it, trying again, and so on.

—DOROTHY PETERS 2000

We have said that before beginning a first project with a group of young children, we spend several weeks building a sense of classroom community. We also spend these weeks involving our students in project-like experiences. As described earlier, the roles of the teacher and the students involved in Applied Learning classrooms are different from many traditional educational experiences. Both teachers and children need opportunities to explore these roles before undertaking a project.

Teachers need opportunities to hone their skills. Being comfortable with facilitating children's discussions and decisions is critical to project work. Guiding children—rather than telling them what to do—often requires rethinking classroom routines and procedures. Incorporating the pondering strategies that scaffold children's learning during project work takes repeated practice. You may need to practice to internalize this different role of guiding, not telling before you introduce a project to your children. Even when the teacher has experience facilitating project work, he or she needs some time with each new group of students to get to know them. Children also need time to become accustomed to a teacher who does not provide "all the answers" and keeps asking them what they think they should do.

It may take a while for children to develop the necessary skills for project work. They need the freedom to plan their own learning experiences, articulate what they are learning, solve problems as a group, and make their own mistakes. While these are high expectations for young children, they are clearly achievable when we provide multiple experiences over several weeks.

From a Kindergarten Teacher . . .

I started my first project in September. It was a flop. Five-year-olds need several weeks, maybe even a month or two, to learn how to work with each other. Few children come into kindergarten knowing how to share and how to take turns, much less how to solve their own conflicts or make group decisions, so now I plan all kinds of activities for children in the first several weeks of school where they work in pairs or in groups of three or four and really learn how to work with each other. We have class meetings every day where we talk about class problems and learn how to make decisions as a whole class. I wait until these things are pretty well in place before I introduce projects to my students, and the first project goes so much more smoothly.

Project work is challenging, and it is much better if both the teacher and the children have experienced project-like activities before launching their first project.

Working Together

Working in groups may be a new experience for some young children. Children who have attended quality early childhood programs will be acquainted with working in groups; however, not all children will have gone to quality programs. Some children in your class will already have learned school "rules" such as no talking when you are working, sharing information is cheating, and asking questions of a peer is not acceptable. These children need time to relearn "school behavior." Recognizing the need to practice working together, we start the school year by implementing pre-project experiences that require working with the entire class and in small groups.

Whole-Class Experiences

We plan our curriculum from the first week of school with an Applied Learning outlook. Children are given simple choices and the class collaborates to produce products. Our early choices and products are not as sophisticated as the ones in true projects, but they are a stepping-stone toward them. For example, we often start our school year with an author study. Either Tana Hoban or Donald Crews appeals to most kindergarten and first-grade children, and second graders like Arnold Lobel's *Frog and Toad* series or Nancy Carlson's stories about Louanne Pig. The children vote, determining which author to study, and we read aloud one or two books each day. As we lead discussions about the various qualities of the books, the children are learning behaviors that are important to project work: listening in a variety of ways, sharing the workload, exploring different points of view, and participating in varied activities. Each day we encourage children to write their own stories and illustrate them. By the end of a week or two, the children are convinced that they are authors and illustrators, and they delight in creating a class book in the author's style.

From a First-Grade Teacher . . .
I like to start the year using Tomie dePaola's series of books about Strega Nona. All children identify with Big Anthony, a mistake-making grown-up. I usually put the Strega Nona books out on the easel and talk about how all the books are about the same people, same place, etc. By the time I'm through, they are dying to hear the story. I read *Strega Nona* first because in it Big Anthony makes a big mistake—he lets pasta cover the town. On subsequent days, we cook pasta, sing the magic song, draw Big Anthony, etc. All the time this is going on I marvel, "You are learning so much about Strega Nona and Big Anthony. I wonder if other classes know this much" and so on. The class comes together over our shared Strega Nona activities.

We treat "theme-like" experiences as pre-projects. "Colors" is often a thematic unit we use at the beginning of the year in kindergarten. In Josh's class, instead of "doing" teacher-prepared activities with colors, he presents the choice to the children by leading a class discussion, "I wonder how many colors are in our baskets? Do you know anything about these colors?" He lists what the children say on a chart tablet, then asks if there is anything that the children would like to know about colors, recording that also. Then he organizes the learning experiences around the children's responses—perhaps mixing colors together, learning songs about the colors, making a color wheel from magazine pictures, etc. The class's learning might be shared with another class who "doesn't know as much as we do" about colors. This begins to establish our Applied Learning outlook of having choices and collaborating to produce products. The children come to expect to have a voice in what they will study and how they will study it.

Working in Pairs or Small Groups

The children's ability to work together is strengthened when they feel competent in their ability and learn to depend on peers for assistance. We structure our classrooms so that children have multiple opportunities to work with partners and small groups. At the beginning of the year when author studies are going on in language arts, shared experiences also happen in other content areas. As first-grade teachers, we would introduce dominoes and set up situations in which small groups of children have to share a set of dominoes to play a math game. We lead class discussions about how to share the materials, and the children come up with techniques. After the lesson, the children review the ways they worked out their problems in their group. We model the expectation that the children will solve their own problems. Of course, it would take less time if we just told the children how to share, but the learning is more authentic and child directed when they do the work. Some of the other paired or small-group experiences we use over the first few weeks of school are outlined here.

PARTNER READING   Even before children become conventional readers, they benefit from "reading" to other people. In partner reading, each child chooses a short book. Together the partners select a quiet place in the room and read their

Figure 4–1.   Partner Reading

books to each other, as shown in Figure 4–1. Most kindergartners can tell stories from the illustrations. Most second graders know how to choose books that they can read conventionally. In either case, this activity helps children learn to listen quietly to another child. This may seem like a minor issue, but young children often find this endeavor quite demanding and one that needs repeated practice.

INDEPENDENT MATH ACTIVITIES These activities are geared for two children, building over a few weeks to games for three or four children. The activities can be simple ones that the teacher created or commercially produced games. They help children learn to take turns; to talk with and depend on each other; and to use language to solve problems. Pairs of kindergarten children could sort a small collection of buttons, keys, or beads while first- and second-grade children might create geometric shapes with pattern blocks. Figure 4–2 shows two girls enjoying math games together.

PARTNER OR SMALL-GROUP DECISIONS Learning to choose among options and develop a rationale for that choice is a responsibility that takes time to develop. In the first

Figure 4–2. Math Games

few weeks of school, we provide numerous opportunities for partners to make decisions. Partners can be assigned the task of choosing the book for the end-of-the-day reading time, selecting the poetry book to be read from after recess, or looking through a list of authors to name the next week's Author of the Week.

PLANNING LEARNING CENTER ACTIVITIES   Small groups of three or four children can be asked to think about several activity options for centers and choose one to set up for the following week. This is a particularly good activity to help you understand how much scaffolding each child needs to generate ideas and how well he or she works with other children in decision making and in carrying out plans agreed to by the group.

PARTNER ASSIGNMENTS FOR CHORES   Rather than assigning one child to take attendance or water plants or care for classroom animals, asking children to work with a partner helps them learn how to divide labor and how to talk to each other about what they have done and what they still need to learn.

From a Second-Grade Teacher . . .

I always thought that I was teaching important skills when I told my students exactly how to do the jobs in our class. I defined the different tasks involved in filling out the lunch count form for the cafeteria, wrote out the seven steps of cleaning the gerbil cage, and posted the rules for cleaning up each learning center in our classroom. I repeated all the procedures day after day until the children learned to do the jobs. Only after talking with some other teachers did I finally realize that telling my students what to do and how to do it was robbing them of important learning experiences. If I wanted them to solve problems during project time, I shouldn't be so directive during other times of the day. I have to admit, I was pretty impressed with their responses when I started asking children, "How do you think you can find all the information the cafeteria needs on this form?" or "How do you think the two of you can best work together to clean this cage?" Sometimes it takes someone else to see how our practices are not exactly promoting the kinds of behaviors we want during projects.

Talking Together

Talk is at the heart of project-based learning. Projects run most effectively and efficiently when the teacher guides children and when children talk to each other using respectful language. At the beginning of the school year, we focus on creating situations in which people in the class talk with each other.

Between Teacher and Child

Perhaps the most important conversations that occur early on are between the teacher and a child. When a teacher focuses on each individual child, remembers small events about his or her life outside of school, and demonstrates genuine affection, that child begins to trust the teacher. That sense of trust is the first step in a good relationship between teacher and child.

From the first day of school, we purposefully make time two or three times a day to talk with children one-on-one. We always start the morning with an informal chat with each child as he or she enters the classroom, asking how they are doing, what they did the night before, or something more personal about their family, pets, or hobbies. Throughout the day, we find two or three minutes to speak with children individually, as they are working in learning centers, during Writers' Workshop, at recess, or at the end of the day. We find that we learn a lot about each child through these conversations, and we believe that these chats are necessary for maintaining good relationships with children.

Among Children

In an effort to get their child to establish friendships, parents often say, "go over to those kids and talk to them." The child reluctantly walks over and stands near the edge of the group for a minute or two. In his or her perception, there is no break in the conversation, no chance to enter in, so he or she goes back to his parents and says, "They won't let me play." In reality, neither the group of children or the new child knew what to say.

Young children need support as they learn the language that helps them build and maintain friendships. We often lead group discussions about different aspects of being a friend. Topics for discussion include "what to say when:"

- You want to join a group.
- Another person takes something you were using.
- Someone hurts you.
- Someone calls you a name.
- Someone hurts your feelings.
- You hurt someone else's feelings.
- You want to borrow something.

These situations are discussed, appropriate phrases are suggested by children, then children role-play the situations while trying out some of the phrases (Denton and Kriete 2000). When one of these situations inevitably comes up in class, we remind the child, or the group of children, what was said during their discussion and role-play about the issue. These small-group discussions with the teacher are just as important as the whole-class discussions. "What works well with young children is individualized guidance . . . Individual focus and the warmth of the interaction increase the child's capacity to hear and respond deeply to the teacher's suggestion" (Katz and McClellan 1997, 20). Through the emphasis on "what to say" to each other, children learn more about friendships and getting along.

We recognize that young children develop friendships and learn social skills over time, so we also reinforce occasions when children are working cooperatively, helping, being polite or respectful, or establishing friendships. Comments such as "Pam, you were respectful of Charlie's ideas when you complimented him," or "Hey, you all worked together to clean up that mess. What a team!" support children's efforts to make friends.

While helping two children develop a friendship is important, project work calls for children to talk with each other about their work. Inevitably, children will have problems. So to help them, we present situations and the children brainstorm possible solutions. They practice these solutions by role-playing. Situations that relate to implementing projects might include "what to say when":

- Your partner is not doing serious work.
- You need help finding materials or resources.
- You need help writing something.
- Nobody in the group volunteers to do what must be done.
- Someone in your group does not read or write as well as others in the group.
- More than one person wants the same job.

As we lead children through these difficult but necessary conversations, we also look for opportunities to teach strategies such as how to ask a question that relates to the ongoing conversation, watching and listening to others' reactions and thoughtfully responding to them, noticing other children's feelings, and being considerate. It is important to note that children's behaviors do not automatically change because of one discussion. It takes many discussions, many reminders of "what we agreed to do," and for some children, many one-on-one conversations with the teacher.

Class Meetings

The group discussions mentioned earlier are different types of class meetings. In the previous chapter, we discussed class meetings to establish class norms and appropriate behavior. Once these types of meetings are firmly established, we begin having class meetings for other purposes: making plans, solving problems, and checking in.

PLANNING MEETINGS   An integral part of an Applied Learning classroom is how the children make decisions about how the project will proceed. Class meetings for making plans involve organizing into groups, reviewing what was accomplished, thinking about next steps, deciding what to work on that day, and so on. During projects, children make day-to-day decisions about how to do the research, document their learning, and share what they have learned. To get children ready to make these larger decisions, we begin with class meetings to discuss producing a whole-class product, such as a class book.

A typical planning meeting in our classrooms begins with a review of what has been accomplished. Then we direct the children's attention to the tasks that need to be done. As always, we approach this with wondering aloud and pondering comments. We ask for the children's input in deciding what tasks should be done next. The children make a decision, and the learning continues. A planning meeting can occur as often as needed. When we are involved in a project, we typically start each project time with a planning meeting.

PROBLEM-SOLVING MEETINGS   We all know that problems occur any place where people work together. This is especially true of classrooms filled with young children. In recognizing this fact, problems are viewed as another teaching opportunity. We lead children through a discussion about their problem and help them reach their own solution, rather than solving their problem for them. For the most part, the problems discussed in class meetings are concerns of the entire class, with issues ranging from sharing community supplies to getting along on the playground. We usually handle a conflict between two or three children privately; however, as the children learn the steps in solving problems, they begin to use that process for working through their own problems (Lantieri and Patti 1996).

We present this five-step process to the children:

1. Tell the problem.
2. Suggest ideas to solve it.
3. Talk about the ideas.
4. Choose one idea.
5. Check the idea.

During problem-solving meetings, children learn how to use language that facilitates solving the problem instead of inflaming it. We teach them how to share their feelings, give reasons to support their opinions, and disagree with an opinion without criticizing the person who expressed it (Schneider 1996).

Sharing Feelings Young children typically label their emotions fairly simply. They are either "sad," "glad," or "mad." We start where children are with these labels. We encourage them to tell other children when someone makes them feel sad or mad. While young children are usually taught to tell the teacher when they have a problem with another child, we encourage children to try first to solve their own problems. We use role-playing to illustrate how to respond to another child's hurtful comments or aggressive behavior. We encourage children to specifically re-state the disliked behavior and suggest I-statements such as:

- "I feel mad when you say my writing is not good."
- "I'm sad when you mark on my drawing. Don't do it again."
- "I don't understand why you push me in line. That makes me very sad. I want you to stop."

When children come to us complaining about another child's behavior, our first response is usually, "What have you already said to him (or her)?" If there was no verbal exchange between the children, we suggest a sentence or two they might say. We only step in to negotiate between children when they have first tried to solve the problem on their own.

From a Kindergarten Teacher . . .

I had one student who had gone to the same child care center since he was a month old. It was a pretty tough center, and Ross had learned that you get attention when you are loud, and you get the toys you want when you take them away from some-body else. Every day we talked about these behaviors and what we expected at our school. Changes in his behaviors were very slow. One afternoon during project time, Ross came up to me complaining that a group of children would not let him sort fos-sils with them. I asked if he had asked to join them. He admitted that he hadn't. He just tried to sit down with them and they kept moving their circle so he didn't have a place to sit. I suggested he go back to the group and say, "Excuse me, could I help you guys sort the fossils? I will share." Moments later, I heard my words being re-peated in a halting sort of way. I turned to work with another child, then the "peace" of the class was broken with Ross' bellowing voice, "Teacher, teacher, it worked. Look, it worked." This was a short interaction between a child and a group that was trying to keep him out. But this incident was the real beginning of Ross's under-standing about asking for what you want from others.

Beyond the sad, glad, and mad identification of the way they feel, we work with children to recognize other emotions they experience. Children need to rec-ognize when they feel frustrated, hurt, or embarrassed, and to learn how to handle those emotions. We help children identify these emotions when we observe them:

- "It seems to me that you are getting frustrated. I've watched you working on this drawing for a long time and it seems like you keep doing this part over and over. Why don't you take a little break and come back to it?"

- "I'll bet you are feeling a little hurt because the boys laughed at your painting. That wasn't how we agreed to react to each other's work. Do you want to tell them how you feel by yourself or do you want me to come along with you?"

Learning to share feelings easily and confront someone who has hurt you or made you mad facilitates project work. When children get used to talking with each other in this way, group work runs more smoothly. So while learning to share feelings is a lifelong skill, it is particularly helpful when children are working on projects.

Supporting Opinions with Reasons Few young children come into school able to support their opinions with valid reasons. Because of their developmental level, they tend to think that whatever they think is fact. This happens with every new group of children we teach. It shows up with the smallest of issues, even selecting what kind of paper they use to record information.

Katherine insisted that everyone in "her" committee use blue paper. Another girl on that committee, Katy, wanted to use big index cards. To adults, this seems like an insignificant problem. To the girls, it was important, and Meredith, their teacher, realized this. She joined the small group and encouraged the girls to share the "why" about what they wanted. Katherine explained that she wanted everybody to use blue paper because "it was the prettiest color paper in the whole room." Katy said she wanted to write on index cards because "they were kind of harder paper and they had lines on them" and she wanted to write on lines. After hearing the reasons why each girl wanted a particular kind of paper, Meredith reminded the girls that everyone in the group did not have to use the same kind of paper, that Katherine could use blue and Katy could use index cards. However, the group did not see that as a solution. They had already agreed to use the same kind of paper for their notes. In a more traditional classroom, a teacher might have said, "Well, it doesn't really matter, so use whatever you want, and quit arguing about it." In Applied Learning classrooms, these small disagreements are teaching and learning opportunities. Meredith tried to get the group to suggest a solution to this problem. This time, the girls did not come up with even one suggestion. Meredith decided to take a strong wondering aloud approach by commenting, "I wonder if there is a way to get "harder" paper with lines that is also blue." She showed the group blue cardstock and offered to copy lines onto the cardstock. The girls readily agreed that that idea was a solution to their problem. The next day, all members of the committee were happily writing notes on their blue, lined cardstock.

This process may seem like a waste of time to some people. To us, this is one way to show children that their opinions are valued and that there is always a solution to a problem. Over time, with experience and the support of their teacher, children learn that they usually do have reasons for what they want, and that others are more willing to listen to "your side" when you share those reasons.

Disagreeing Without Criticizing   One of the fastest ways to end a conversation is to make fun of someone's idea or to criticize the person who offers the idea. Trying to get young children to understand this concept takes time. Many children tend to call names when they disagree with somebody or something. "You're just a dummy," is not an unusual comment when two young children are disagreeing with each other. We find ourselves repeating statements like, "How would you feel if Jack said the very same thing you just said to him?" many times in those first few weeks of school. We mediate similar discussions throughout the day—on the playground, waiting in line in the cafeteria, working on math games, and any number of other situations.

We present situations during class meetings and ask the children to role-play how to handle situations when they disagree with someone. The entire group can suggest effective language to use rather than name calling or using any other form of criticizing. It is important to note that children can role-play these situations and demonstrate appropriate behavior during class meetings before they internalize the concept of respectful interactions. Still, we believe that it is worth the time spent in class meetings and in personal conversations with individual children to help the class learn to share their feelings, give reasons to support their opinions, and disagree with an opinion without criticizing the person who expressed it.

CHECK-IN MEETINGS   Check-in meetings are opportunities to talk about small-group or whole-class issues. They occur at any time during the day. For some check-in meetings, children and the teacher meet for a brief time to make sure that everyone has a plan for that project time or, perhaps, to ensure that every committee has materials they need. Other check-in meetings are used to evaluate something related to the class—how well everyone is getting along, how parts of the project are going, how a solution to a particular problem is working.

As a self-assessment tool, check-in meetings focus the group's attention on how well they are following class norms, meeting class plans, or evaluating solutions to problems (Developmental Studies Center 1996). Reviewing the final question of the problem-solving guidelines—how did our idea work?—is critically important. When we give children the opportunity to revisit their solutions and consider how well their solutions are working, they learn from those decisions.

Not only do check-in meetings facilitate this self-assessment, but they can also be used to evaluate the progress of a project. The whole class might check their progress toward a class deadline or determine if more time is needed. After completing a project's end product, the children also use check-in meetings to evaluate all aspects of that product.

Summary

Pre-project experiences prepare children and teachers for the roles that they will assume during actual projects. Working in groups and talking with peers in respectful ways are behaviors that teachers teach explicitly. Children need multiple experiences with these behaviors before they can be expected to work together successfully.

5

Getting Started

I believe the ultimate in education is reached when learners—both students and teachers at all levels—take charge of their own learning and use their education to lead rich and satisfying lives. That is, as learners, they are able to inquire independently about everything that interests them, choose to read and write for their own purposes, find and use resources to seek the knowledge and information they desire, write to learn, reflect, think, modify their thinking, and take new action. Further, they constantly set goals for themselves, self-evaluate, seek feedback, and go on learning. Even very young children can do this—and they do, when teachers and other experts (such as parents and fellow students) serve as models and mentors.

—REGIE ROUTMAN 1996

The Right Time for a Project

You've spent the first few weeks of school creating a sense of community among your students and working through different pre-project experiences. Classroom routines are in place, and the children seem to be coming together as a group. Now it is time to think about starting the first project with your class. But, how do you know the time is right?

There is no magic formula to determine when to start a first project. There is no way to know for sure, but you can feel reasonably certain that the children are ready when they are behaving in certain ways—most of the time—and you feel ready to try teacher roles that support child-directed work.

Child Behaviors Important for Project Work
- Engaging in self-selected literacy activities
- Working cooperatively in pairs and small groups

- Making decisions about what to work on during self-selected center time
- Asking questions related to one topic
- Talking through interpersonal problems

Teacher Roles Important for Project Work
- Encouraging children to make decisions about their work
- Guiding children without telling them what to do
- Using pondering strategies to lead children
- Locating and providing multiple resources for a single topic
- Feeling at ease not knowing how a project will end

There will never be a time when every student demonstrates all of these behaviors, and you may never feel equally comfortable with each of the teacher roles. These are not reasons to wait. Believing in the potential of project-based learning and observing most of the child behaviors and teacher roles are reason enough to try a project.

Components of Applied Learning Projects

There are four major components in Applied Learning projects. The first component is selecting the topic to study. The second component is planning the project. This includes creating shared knowledge about the topic, posing questions, and deciding how to proceed. The third component is implementing plans for the project, including finding and using resources and organizing the information that the children are learning. The fourth component is choosing and creating an end product that shares knowledge with other people.

This description of the Rock and Fossil Exhibit project highlights the four components in project work:

Reading *Everybody Needs a Rock* (1974), by Byrd Baylor, inspired children to hunt for their own special rocks on the playground. Deborah's students approached this decision very seriously. Each made little piles of rocks then sorted through them until the pile was narrowed down to one rock. Back in the classroom, Deborah modeled how to write a scientific collection label for her rock and placed the rock with its label in the science center. The children followed her lead, using developmental spelling. She thought she had taken advantage of a teachable moment, but that was not the end of the experience with rocks.

Rocks seemed to capture the class's attention. Within days, more than one hundred rocks were on science center shelves, and the children were asking more questions about rocks than Deborah could answer. During a class meeting, she suggested the class consider the topic of rocks for the next inquiry, and called for a class vote. Within minutes, the children had decided to study rocks (component one of project work: selecting a topic).

In that same class meeting, Deborah suggested they start a KWL chart (component two: planning the project). The class had done this before, so the process was familiar. The KWL chart launched the research. Over the next few weeks, the children researched and documented their learning about rocks and fossils during project time. They collected books about rocks, looked up Internet sites, located experts and asked them questions, made lists of facts, brought in rocks to add to their collection, and went on a class field trip so they could collect fossils (component three: implementing the plan). Within each activity, Deborah taught literacy, math, and science skills, and the children learned new skills, improved skills they already had, and picked up new facts every day. Soon, the children began to see themselves as experts about rocks and fossils.

At this point, Deborah suggested that "This class knows more about rocks than any class in the school. How could we share what we've learned with other people?" The children had not been involved in projects before, so they were not really sure what this meant. In kind of a pondering way, Deborah mentioned visiting the geology hall at a local museum and asked the class if they could make a rock and fossil exhibit like the people at the museum made. There was a resounding "yes."

With that decision, their focus during project time changed from research to deciding how to create an exhibit (component four: choosing and creating an end product). During the next couple of weeks, the class took a field trip to the museum to see how adults created an exhibit about rocks, talked to the museum staff about signage, wrote facts and drew pictures to hang in the museum, drafted label copy for their rocks and fossils, and created an exhibit brochure. Students also planned and carried out a successful museum opening for friends and families. Their organized tours of the exhibit were popular with the other classes in the school. These activities also called for new learning (writing informative paragraphs, writing scientific labels, using field guides to identify rocks and fossils, sending email messages). During each part of creating the exhibit, Deborah extended the children's literacy, math, and science skills.

Selecting a Topic

The first component of an Applied Learning project is selecting the topic. This decision does not always happen as easily as it did in the Rocks and Fossils Exhibit project. Sometimes the topic for a project comes directly from an interest of the children, but choosing a topic can happen in several different ways (Diffily 1996). A topic might come from a class brainstorming session, a suggestion from you or another adult, or a curriculum topic.

While you may make suggestions, the children make the actual decision about what the topic of a project will be. By the time our classes start working on a project, we've led them through many pre-project experiences in making group decisions. They have learned about voting and reaching consensus.

> **From a Kindergarten Teacher . . .**
> When I started my first project, I was really worried about leaving so many important decisions in the hands of young children. But after a year of project work, I have to say I am pretty amazed at some of their decisions. There were times during the year when they would make a decision, and I would think, "Oh, no, how are we going to get through this one?" and then I would watch them work it out. Young children can be awfully impressive if we just give them the opportunities to show us what they can do.

Planning a Project

The second component is planning the project. This initial stage of planning for a project does not last very long. Typically, you start the planning process by leading children into listing what they know about a topic and what they want to learn by using a KWL chart. You may guide them into making some predictions about some of the questions or may move directly into trying to confirm the "facts" they stated (young children list misinformation as fact at the beginning of an inquiry) and trying to find answers to questions.

WHAT WE KNOW   On the first day of the Rocks and Fossils Exhibit project, children dictated what they knew about rocks:

- "Some rocks are little."
- "Some rocks are big."
- "Some rocks are white and some rocks are colors."
- "Some rocks are heavy, but I can pick them up."
- "We have little rocks on the playground."
- "My dad calls playground rocks gravel."
- "My dad got me an ammonite."
- "Ammonites are special rocks."
- "I got a lot of rocks in my bedroom."
- "We have a lot of rocks in the science center."

WHAT WE WANT TO LEARN   The "What We Want to Learn" chart is shown in Figure 5–1. Some of the questions children dictated were:

- "Does all dirt look the same?"
- "What is dirt? Is it soil?"
- "How are rocks alike?"
- "How are rocks different?"
- "Can plants grow in rocks?"

It is important to note that young children do not always distinguish between a statement and a question. We often switch back and forth between writing on the *K* part of the KWL chart and the *W* part of the chart depending on what a child says. Virtually every time we take dictation from young children, some will dictate "facts" even though the class has moved on to dictating "What We Want to Know."

In this project, as is true for most projects we've done with young children, there was not a lot of prior knowledge about the topic. In fact, many of the kindergartners were still developing the concept of "fact." On their KWL chart, most children made random statements about rocks. Even as a group of twenty-two, they did not have that many questions. It would have been easy for Deborah to think, "If they only have five questions about rocks, should I even pursue this?

Figure 5–1. "What We Want to Learn" Chart

Maybe I should look for another topic." But this was a beginning. Deborah knew her students were interested in the topic because of the number of rocks that were brought into the classroom, the way they sorted their rocks and talked about them, and the drawings and writing about rocks that the children created during Writers' Workshop. So the work continued.

As soon as several questions have been posed, the research component begins. However, planning does not stop here. The children continue to plan throughout the research and the creation of the end product. Helping children record their plans keeps the project on track. In the Rocks and Fossils Exhibit project, Deborah transcribed a running "to do" list for the class. As shown in Figure 5–2, they crossed off the things they had done, and Deborah added new things that needed doing as the children identified them.

Implementing the Plan

Just as planning for a project is a process that weaves itself throughout the entire project, the same thing happens with research. You never quite know where the research will lead. The children start looking for answers to their questions, but

Figure 5–2.   Children Checking "To Do" List

through read-alouds and their own research, new questions come up. It seems that the more the children learn, the more questions they have. So the research process affects the planning as much as the planning drives the research.

FINDING AND USING RESOURCES   The third component begins with finding and using all kinds of resources. Children may bring in books or artifacts and, with help from their families, even locate experts to answer some of the questions. But teachers do not depend only on students' abilities to locate resources. While the support that children need during a project cannot be anticipated, you can start looking for resources for the children to use as soon as the topic is set. The teacher provides extra resources to round out the research process—a school library usually has limited nonfiction books on a single topic. So Applied Learning teachers borrow books from other teachers; go to the public library and local bookstores; or ask friends, and friends of friends, if they would be willing to serve as experts for classes. Also, teachers might propose field trip opportunities.

While we want children to find resources, we don't expect them to know how to go about doing this during initial projects. This is something they have to learn. As teachers introduce the concept of projects to students, the pondering strategy is used rather strongly to lead children into thinking about how they might help locate resources. Children may need guidance through comments such as, "Ryan, isn't your mom a landscape architect? I'll bet she knows a lot about what kinds of rocks can be found in our town. Do you think she might help us find information about rocks?" or "Yolanda, doesn't your sister volunteer at the City Gardens? I'll bet she knows something about the rocks at the gardens. She might come to our class and answer questions if we wrote a letter to her."

Young children's research is different from that of older students. Applied Learning teachers introduce three ways to conduct research:

- Books and other printed materials
- Observation
- Asking questions of an expert

Children might read a caption, note a heading, or listen while a passage is read aloud. They could measure the growth of a plant, writing the numbers in a log. They might draw the changes they observe or listen to an expert.

The research for the Rocks and Fossils Exhibit project began with children looking through the books that Deborah had read aloud and at photographs of rocks in books that had text too complicated for them to read. Some children chose to observe the rocks that we had in the science center. They examined the rocks with magnifying glasses and grouped rocks that looked alike. Other children decided to write letters to the two "experts" that Deborah had told them about.

Our belief about student-directed projects allows children to research the topic in whatever ways they choose.

DOCUMENTING THE LEARNING The third component of project work continues with the children documenting what they are learning. Although children are held responsible for documenting their research, they have choices about how and what to document. Each child keeps a record of what he or she is learning during the research process. Every child's documentation looks different, because the quality of it depends on the literacy ability of each child.

We encourage children to record some kind of learning every day. However, young children learn much more than they are capable of documenting. During the Rocks and Fossils Exhibit project, a group of children listened to an audiotape called *Fossils Tell of Long Ago* (Aliki 1990). The book was filled with information about fossils. Yet, when making notes for their research folders, one child drew a picture of an ammonite, one wrote: FASL R RKS, and the third child asked if he could sketch the front cover of the book. During our class meeting, these children orally contributed several facts they had learned, proving that they had learned and retained much more than their documentation showed.

The kindergartners in the Rocks and Fossils Exhibit project documented their learning in different ways:

- Drawings
- Fact cards
- Answers to questions posted on the KWL chart
- Photocopied pages from books, magazines, and Internet sites
- Copies of their letters and the responses they received
- Email messages

Some of the work samples are shown in Figures 5–3a–c.

As children conducted their research and recorded what they were learning, Deborah circulated through the classroom. She worked with individual children and small groups. On any given day, she might offer a tip on researching, refer one child to another who was looking for an answer to the same question, or teach a particular reading or writing strategy. This approach of working with small groups of children continued through to the end product component.

Choosing and Creating an End Product

Choosing and creating an end product is the final component of Applied Learning projects. This end product illustrates what our students learn during their research. Applied Learning end products are created using a model and are designed

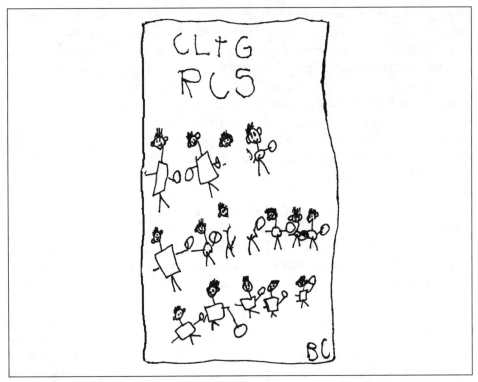

Figure 5–3a. Work Sample from Rock and Fossil Exhibit Project, "Collecting Rocks."

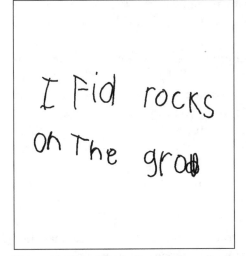

Figure 5–3b. Work Sample from Rock and Fossil Exhibit Project, "I found rocks on the ground."

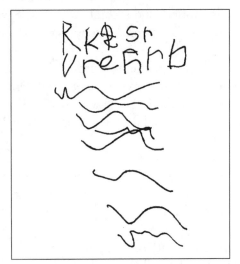

Figure 5–3c. Work Sample from Rock and Fossil Exhibit Project, "Rocks are hard."

for a specific audience. The model is often something created by an adult expert—the local science museum's displays, the zoo's informational signs, a brochure created to inform parents about the benefits of reading aloud to children, etc. Children need to pattern their work after the best possible example.

Children also consider their audience as they create the end product. When planning the Rock and Fossil Exhibit, the children considered what appealed to elementary-age students—bright colors, easy-to-read words, borders, etc. As planning began for informational signs in the Outdoor Learning Environment, the children considered how to best give information to the school's adult neighbors who would be visiting the area, their younger siblings who would play there, and the other children in the school.

The end product could be an informational video, an informational brochure, a nonfiction book, a how-to manual, a museum exhibit, a vegetable garden, a board game, or a number of others. Because projects are tied to the real world, we want children to understand that they can produce products similar to ones they see in bookstores, museums, zoos, and retail stores. Appendix C lists a variety of possible end products.

SELECTING A PRODUCT Children who have not had previous experiences with Applied Learning need help in recognizing the possible ways to share their learning. One of the most effective ponderings we use with young children at this stage of projects is, "I wonder if we could _____ (write a book, make a brochure, create an exhibit, etc.) like the fifth graders did?" Children in kindergarten, first, and second grade always want to emulate the things that "the big kids" do. This works in schools where classes at other grade levels are also involved in projects.

If you are the only project-based teacher in an elementary school, your ponderings would take a slightly different direction. You might say, "Ms. Watkins made a bulletin board with her students' work about Native Americans. Do you think we could do something like that? How do you think we should start?" Or, you could connect it to the school's Science or History Fair by saying, "Remember when we went to the library to see the Science Fair? There were all those backboards filled with information. Do you think that would be a good way to let other people in the school know what we know about rocks?" Once an end product has been selected, we find a model the children can use as a guide.

USING A MODEL If children are going to create products similar to ones they find in the real world, they must have competent models to examine. We agree that it is unrealistic to ask young children to create a product that looks like something created by an adult. However, when we teach children to read and write, we always use models of good writing by adults. In Applied Learning end products, we use competent models in the same way. If children are going to create an exhibit, they need to see examples of good exhibits. We do not expect young children to replicate the adult models, but to approximate them at their level—by looking at the model, describing the good characteristics of the model, and trying to incorporate those characteristics into their end product. Just as children use adult models of books to write their own books, children working on Applied Learning projects use adult models to create their end products.

When they made the decision to make an exhibit, Deborah arranged a field trip to the science and history museum. In the geology hall, she led a discussion about what made the exhibit good. Students listed several different characteristics. As they were working on their own exhibit, Deborah often reminded students to remember those characteristics. At the end of the project, Deborah and her students evaluated their exhibit based on how well their work met their list of the characteristics of a good exhibit.

CONSIDERING THE AUDIENCE   Identifying the audience for an Applied Learning project is an important element of the end product. Considering a specific audience is also important in the writing process (Zinsser 1998), so your students may already be familiar with this concept before they start project work.

For the kindergartners working on the Rocks and Fossils Exhibit project, the audience was not obvious to the children. As young children research new information, they naturally seem to want to share it with everyone "who doesn't know as much as we do." In the case of the exhibit, the audience that was finally selected was other classes in the school. The audience might have been children who are even younger than they are, other classes at their grade level, family members, friends of the class or the school, visitors to the school, or community members.

Project Timeline

For all projects, these components will require different amounts of time. The Rocks and Fossils Exhibit project lasted seven weeks. For five and a half weeks, the children worked on the project for approximately an hour a day. The final week and a half were spent giving exhibit tours. This was a first project for this class, and first projects always seem to take more time than subsequent projects. This week-by-week timeline gives an idea how this project proceeded.

Timeline for Rocks and Fossils Exhibit Project
- **Week One**—Vote to study rocks, begin KWL chart, read aloud books about rocks to the whole class, start listing possible resources, begin sorting rocks in science center, start independent research, begin collecting documenta-

tion of what is learned and storing it in pocket folders, use field guides to identify some of the more obvious rock types, write facts, draw pictures of rocks, write letters to experts.

- **Week Two**—Continue adding to KWL chart, begin reading downloaded information from Internet sites, children begin talking about "volcano rocks," look for information about rocks created by volcanoes, continue writing facts about rocks and drawing pictures, write more letters to experts, mark pages of books and articles to be photocopied for project folders.

- **Week Three**—Decision to create a museum exhibit; plan field trip to see exhibit of rocks and fossils; continue writing facts about rocks and marking pages of books and articles to be photocopied for project folders; create pictures of rocks using different media; expand writing to include stories, books, and poems; start mural showing geologists collecting rocks.

- **Week Four**—Continue adding to KWL chart, go on field trip to science museum, decide to add fossils to exhibit, begin research about fossils, dictate "Important Facts About Rocks," measure the room to be used for the exhibit, make floor plans, arrange furniture, discuss and make lists of what should be included in the exhibit, decide how museum should be arranged, plan museum opening, create and send out invitations to opening, create and distribute memo inviting classes in school to schedule a tour of the exhibit, draft exhibit brochure copy, weekend field trip to collect more fossils.

- **Week Five**—Write letters to borrow "volcano rocks" from the science museum to display, create more pictures of rocks using various media, hang these pictures as pictorial display (like the children had seen at the museum) for the entrance to the exhibit, build and paint stands for each child's favorite rock, finalize brochure, make copies of brochure.

- **Week Six**—Create "Guess What This Rock Is" display, finish hanging facts and pictures, set up rock and fossil collection with labels, hold museum opening for families and special friends of the class, give tours to other classes in the school.

- **Week Seven**—Give tours to other classes and visitors to the school.

Issues to Consider When Implementing Projects

The previous sections in this chapter talked about the components of Applied Learning projects. There is no way to describe exactly how each component of a project will play out because there are simply too many factors that are different from project to project. A project's progress is influenced by the topic, the number of resources located, the end product, the decisions your students make, and your own actions. We can't give a "book of answers" for implementing projects; however, the remainder of this chapter offers advice for you to consider as you think about a first project. In looking back on our first year or two of implementing projects with children, these are things we wished someone had told us.

Choosing a High-Interest Topic

Young children who have never been involved in a project are not typically good sources for topic ideas. There are times when a brainstorming session and voting work well and a topic naturally emerges. More often, you will decide the topic for a first project, and then use the pondering strategy to lead children in a discussion about projects and that topic. If done well, the children will feel that they made the decision.

This may sound manipulative to some people. We don't see it this way. The point of letting young children believe they made the decision about a topic to study is to help them see themselves as empowered decision makers from the beginning of a project. Truly letting children choose the topic for a project without any adult guidance may be setting them up for failure. There may not be enough resources to support a project. It may be impractical. It may not be appropriate for school.

You know topics that generally appeal to students in kindergarten, first, or second grade. Many of the topics used in thematic units can be used in projects. These include:

- Families
- Celebrations
- Their class
- Their school
- Their community
- All kinds of animals
- Weather topics such as rain, tornadoes, hurricanes
- Planting and caring for plants

While these topics can be used for projects, it is important to remember not to lapse back into the traditional ways you organized thematic units. Keep in mind the characteristics and components of projects, especially the characteristic of projects being student directed. Even when you select the topic, always keep in mind the need for the children to feel ownership of project decisions.

Starting Small

Being ambitious is not particularly good for a first project. It is better to start with something small, a project that is fairly limited in time, cost, and end product. The museum exhibit we describe in this chapter may sound very interesting. Children acquire significant knowledge and skills when they research a topic and create an exhibit for other people to view. But nothing says that a museum exhibit is a better way for children to share what they have learned than something less complex. For a first project, it might be just as effective—and certainly less time-consuming—if the students create posterboard displays, hang them in the classroom or in the hallway, and invite other classes to see their displays. Starting with a small project lets you and the students go through the processes related to project work without encountering as many roadblocks as might be involved in more complex projects.

In Chapter 1, the characteristics of a project were listed and discussed. When you think about these characteristics—student directed, connected to the real world, research based, informed by multiple resources, embedded with knowledge and skills, conducted over time, and concluded with an end product—several topics may come to mind. Something as simple as researching and planting a small garden (see Figure 5–4) easily includes all the characteristics of a project. All of these characteristics could be met easily through a project about gardens, but if any one characteristic is overlooked or ignored, what might be a rigorous Applied Learning project becomes a simple study of gardens or plants. Other small projects that might be good "first" projects are discussed Appendix D.

Leading Decisions

Children who have not had many experiences making decisions will not automatically begin making good decisions just because they are given that opportunity.

From a Second-Grade Teacher . . .
My first project was disastrous. I had been reading about projects and thought they sounded like a great learning experience. We had just finished a study of the water cycle and I was sure that this would make a good first project. I had a group meeting

Figure 5–4.   Chad Caring for Plants

with my second graders and talked to them about projects. I told them since we had already done the research component, we could just plan and do the end product, which I suggested be an exhibit for the hall. They all agreed with my suggestions, and I could hardly wait to watch what would happen next. The next day we talked about different areas of information that should be included in the exhibit, then the children divided into groups and started working on some posters to display. This went on for three or four days. I was so disappointed. Their work was sloppy, not just typical of second graders, but just plain sloppy. There was no organization to the information. It seemed like they were just writing random facts. By stepping back, and through talking to a teacher friend of mine who had read the same articles, I realized that the project was not going well because of mistakes I made. The children didn't buy into this idea. They didn't really want to create this exhibit. I learned an important lesson. I told the children what we were going to do. I approached the whole thing wrong. I didn't give up on projects, but you can be sure that I did things differently the next time.

After the children learn some of the skills required for decision making—weighing options, stating a rationale for opinions, considering another point of view, negotiating, and compromising—project work is more successful. Through pre-project experiences and creating situations in which children make decisions, you are preparing children for project work—and teaching them decision-making skills they will use for the rest of their lives.

Trusting the Children's Decisions

It is hard to break the old, seemingly universal arrangement where adults know what is best and children follow their direction. In some cases, that old adage is still true, for example, in safety issues or when there is no time for a group meeting and a quick decision is needed. However, most of the time, children make good decisions when the question is framed appropriately and they have adequate preparation. Sometimes children come up with ideas that adults would never think of. Given a rich environment and the empowerment to make decisions, children make some very interesting decisions.

From a First-Grade Teacher . . .

Three children were drafting an answer to a letter from a parent who had offered to help the class with a science experiment. I helped them edit their paper and asked them how they were going to share the work of writing the final draft. They replied, "We decided to each write." When I asked what that meant, Emily explained, "Tarren will write the first three words, Jimmy does the next three, then I do the next three. You know, we *each write*." This was not a solution I would have thought of, and it did not make very much sense to me. But it worked well for these children.

It is hard to give up the decisions that you've always made in class and let the children make them. Sometimes children are just not able to make good decisions. Still, if children are going to learn to make decisions, they must have lots of opportunities to do just that.

In responding to children's decision making, it is important to remember that they are young. They are just beginning to learn how to contemplate choices and state reasons for their preferences. We support children as they are learning decision-making skills, even if they appear, to us, to be "bad" decisions.

Influencing Children's "Bad" Decisions

Sometimes a decision makes perfect sense to five-, six- or seven-year-olds and we just can't understand it. We have to decide if the decision is one we should try to reverse, or if it really doesn't matter from an educational perspective.

Every so often, children make decisions that are clearly impossible to implement. The children who created the Rock and Fossil Exhibit loved the attention they received when they opened their exhibit, so later in the year, they decided that they wanted to study giraffes and create another exhibit. They were convinced that an exhibit featuring a real giraffe would be "so much better than just having rocks and fossils." Of course, Deborah knew that there was no way the class could make that happen. Still, rather than announcing that securing a live giraffe would be impossible and that they would have to come up with another plan, she tried to lead the children into realizing the impracticality of their decision.

Deborah decided to lead children into an area of research that might help them reconsider their decision. She opened the next class meeting by mentioning, "Okay, let's think about this. It seems to me that when I was at the zoo, the giraffes were a whole lot taller than I. I wonder how tall a giraffe really is. How could we find out?" After a few minutes of discussion among the children, she commented, "Oh wait. I just thought of something. How tall is the room where we would put the museum? We are going to have to measure that too, aren't we? How could we do that?"

In this situation, a seemingly "bad" decision on the part of the children was quickly reversed. A small group of children went to the library and came back with the information that giraffes are generally twelve to fifteen feet tall. Other children found the school custodian and came back with the information that the museum space had an eight-foot ceiling. It only took a few minutes for the children to compare the two quantities and decide that they could not put a real giraffe in the museum. It took three more class meetings, and Deborah's continued "wonderings," for the class to decide against their next choices of a bear museum, a cheetah museum, and a monkey museum. It took another day for the children to come to the decision to study ladybugs, with one of the deciding factors being "they're small enough to put lots in the museum." Trying to lead the children away from a seemingly "bad" decision is not a matter of not trusting the children, but one of guiding them into making good decisions, into taking a problem and finding a workable solution.

From a Second-Grade Teacher . . .

I used to pride myself in being able to solve all the children's problems. I thought I was helping children see that there is a solution to every problem, but I was always the one with the solution. "Let Jonathan play in the sand center first, then it can be your turn." "Let's divide the markers so you'll each have your own colors and you won't have to argue over markers." I've learned through project work that children can solve most of their problems, if I just hold back a little. Now I ask more questions, such as, "What are some ways you can resolve this argument?" "What could you do differently next time to keep this from happening again?" and "I'm not sure. What do you think?" My role as a problem solver is just as important as before, but now I guide the children and trust that they will come up with solutions to their own problems. I really think I am teaching more now than I was before.

Mediating Arguments

Everything does not always run smoothly in project work. Young children often have strong opinions about what "ought to be done." They are still learning how to express opinions and justifying them with reasons. Learning how to handle these kinds of problems is just as valuable as learning specific content knowledge.

At one point in the Rocks and Fossils Exhibit project, several children had an argument about which facts should be included in the exhibit. Some of the more sophisticated children tried to exclude some of the facts dictated by less experienced students. For a class meeting, Deborah gathered a few books about rocks and read aloud from parts of each book. Several statements in the books seemed to be contradictory. The class talked about how authors write what they know and that every author has the right to do that. During that discussion, every child stated his or her opinion about the conflict. When the vote was taken, it was nineteen to three to post everyone's facts because authors do not always agree. The exhibit opened with signs that read "Rocks can't walk," and "Rocks cannot talk to each other." Some parents giggled when they read those facts about rocks, but had to concede that the facts were, indeed, true.

Sometimes it is hard to sit through these discussions. With the deadline of the exhibit opening coming up quickly (they had already made posters announcing the first day visitors could come to the exhibit) it would have been so much easier if Deborah had just said, "Now, it's only fair for everyone to have their dictated facts hung in the museum." However, that would have short-changed the children's learning. Settling arguments is part of everyday living, so it was important to facilitate the children's consideration of this conflict and decision about the problem.

From a Kindergarten Teacher . . .

I'm often not sure if I should support the children's decisions or redirect them. Working with children on projects reminds me of a dance between teacher and students. Sometimes one leads, sometimes the other. Sometimes the situation calls for slow, meticulous steps. Other times the steps are fast and complex. Neither type of dancing is right or wrong, it's just that different music calls for different types of dancing.

The same is true of teachers and students working together on projects. Both make decisions that seem best at the time, considering the situation at hand. I had to give up making the "right" decisions and learn to trust that the children and I were making the best decisions at the time.

Summary

Starting a first Applied Learning project is not an easy task. The four major components in Applied Learning projects are selecting the topic to study, planning the project, implementing plans for the project, and choosing and creating an end product that shares knowledge with other people. You probably have many questions about project work. While there are guidelines that Applied Learning teachers use to make decisions, there are no clear-cut answers for every situation that arises. Still, the intellectual and social gains evident in the children who participate in Applied Learning projects are worth the uncertain moments that project work can bring.

6

Your First Project

Projects provide contexts in which children's curiosity can be expressed purposefully, and that enable them to experience the joy of self-motivated learning.
—Judy Harris Helm and Lilian Katz 2001

This chapter highlights our roles as teachers as we work with children to plan and implement Applied Learning projects. It begins by discussing how to get a project started and continues through all phases of a project following the same four components introduced in Chapter 5—selecting a topic, planning the project, conducting research, and producing a final product.

Starting a Project

Projects are research based, so topic selection usually starts with something the children want to know more about. Children who have never experienced making decisions about what they will study need guidance in choosing their first, and probably their second or third project topic. To get ideas for projects that the whole class buys into, teachers use children's interests, ask for suggestions from the children in brainstorming sessions, expand the interest of one child, or enhance a parent's suggestion.

Ideas from Children's Interests

Young children can come up with very unconventional topics that they want to know more about. Many of these suggestions are not appropriate for Applied Learning projects. Young children are interested by mass media action figures, but these would not be appropriate topics for projects. If the topic is too broad, too narrow, or inappropriate for school, then the teacher's pondering or reflecting can help guide the children's choice. Topics that are not appropriate for projects can be addressed in other ways. For example, the children who wanted to study "kicking the soccer ball," formed an Interest Club that met during center time. This topic might have become a class project if there had been enough interest among their classmates. In this case, only a few children were interested for a few days. The group engaged in some project-like activities (the teacher talked with the children about soccer, they consulted soccer books, the PE teacher came in for a demonstration lesson about kicking, and so on) that might have led to a project, but it did not.

A CLASS BRAINSTORMING SESSION   When Deborah led a class meeting to find out what her first-grade students wanted to study, among the responses were: tying shoes, making beds, and doing cartwheels. None of these topics lend themselves to project work. What would the learning be? What would possible research resources be? Where could any of these ideas lead?

Rather than just announce that these were not good topics, Deborah began questioning the children, making comments like, "Most children in our class can already tie shoes. Should the whole class spend time studying something that we can already do? Have you ever seen a book about making beds? What would we learn if we studied cartwheels?" Through the answers to these questions and the conversations that followed, the children voted to keep thinking about new topics. After three days of class meetings about this issue, making lists and discussing their merits, this class voted to study the topic of reptiles. The children knew something about reptiles. They had observed and cared for their science center's pet turtle and pet snake for four months. It was a topic that virtually all the children found interesting and thought they could find information about. They could start with the knowledge they had gained through observation, search through resources to learn more about reptiles, and culminate the project with a museum exhibit about reptiles.

AN INDIVIDUAL CHILD'S INTEREST   A project might be started by an object that a child brings from home. In Linda's second-grade class, Drew brought Kachina dolls from her family's collection. This led, after many class meetings and discussions, to setting up a hallway exhibit to illustrate Navajo customs. Often one child's interest is already shared by other children in the class.

Offering opportunities for children to share their interests sparks projects. This sharing extends further than traditional "show and tell" that may occur on one day each week. We structure share time within scheduled class meetings, designate areas of the room for displaying items, or set up small group share sessions during the day. Any of these methods for sharing a personal interest could lead to an Applied Learning project.

A PARENT'S CONTRIBUTION   Parents' interests or contributions to the class can also lead to a project. Mike, the parent of a kindergarten child, knew that his child's class had been discussing the rain forest. He accompanied the class when they went to a botanical conservatory, trying to identify different jungle plants and reading *The Great Kapok Tree* by Lynne Cherry (1990) while sitting among the large plants. When he saw a newspaper advertisement about something called "The Children's Rainforest," he sent it to school. The children listened quietly as Deborah read about a conservation effort in Costa Rica. For a contribution of $100, an acre of the rain forest would be protected. This information led to a class decision to write an informational brochure about protecting the rain forest and a fund-raising plan to raise the required $100.

Of course, this kind of involvement from families comes only when teachers keep families informed about the class's activities and maintain a friendly, open-door policy in the classroom. If families are going to contribute to the life of a class, they must know what is going on within the classroom (Gorham and Nason 1997). A brief discussion of ways to involve families is included in Appendix E.

Topics to Cover the Curriculum

Topics for projects can also come from a need in the curriculum (Katz and Chard 2000). If the curriculum mandates that first-grade children learn certain things about rocks, then we create interest for that topic by having rock specimens in the science center and trade books about rocks in the reading center. We watch and listen for the first graders' involvement and then, in our best "pondering" way, ask, "Would you like to learn more about rocks? Could you add that topic to our list of things we want to learn?" If children's interest is piqued, then rocks might evolve into a project. If it doesn't, we don't worry. Rocks—or any other topic—can be studied in a different way.

In the Bat Display project, Charlotte knew that a field trip to see the zoo's temporary exhibit about bats was planned for all the classes in the school. She noticed children watching birds one day on the playground. Knowing about the bat exhibit, she mused, "Did you know that bats are not birds?" The resulting conversation sparked the children's natural curiosity and launched the project.

A teacher might mention to a few students that, "I noticed that there are three trees out in front of the school. What do you guys know about trees and leaves? I wonder if all trees are the same, just leaves and branches? How do trees grow? Would you be interested in finding out?"

Joe led his second-grade students into choosing to create math games for the school's Math-O-Ween event. Using his best pondering voice, and repeating the phrase, "I wonder if we might—," eventually the class voted to research board games and create their own board games for Math-O-Ween. Children divided themselves into pairs or groups of three. Within less than three weeks, the class was ready for the event with six different games:

- Geometry Dilemma
- Mental Math
- Matching Shapes and Colors
- Math Tools
- Graphing Answers
- Problem-Solving Strategies
- All Kinds of Math

Without realizing it, the children met fourteen of the math standards mandated by their school district.

It is important to restate that teachers do not announce topics for projects to the children. The children must be a part of the decision-making process about all project topics. Teachers find different ways to plant the seed of a project in children's minds. As children become aware of their surroundings and their power to make decisions, finding topics for projects gets easier.

Topics from a Teacher's Informal Actions

Just as topics can develop from interests of the children or a particular topic in the curriculum, ideas for topics can be generated in other ways. Informal collaborations among project-based teachers or conversations with children can prompt projects.

ANOTHER ADULT PRESENTS A CONCERN   A teacher might ask a colleague or administrator to voice a concern to the class. Charlotte asked the principal to talk to her class about an area of the school that looked rather dreary. Maria dropped by Charlotte's kindergarten class later that day and remarked, "The area around the side entrance of the school looks so plain and bare compared to the front door that has all the flower beds and native plants. Could the class do something about the way it looks?" The result of this suggestion was the Plants in Containers project. The end products were decorative concrete urns planted and placed near the entrance and a manual about growing plants in containers for the school's library.

Children can also take on responsibilities normally handled by adults in school settings. For example, when Maria received the notice about the school district's annual canned food drive for the local food bank, she offered it to the classes (instead of the teachers) as a possible project. Three first-grade classes joined together to shape the project. The children made advertising signs; designed ways to encourage donations; collected, counted, and sorted the cans; and created a how-to manual for other schools interested in letting children run the drive.

TEACHERS ACTIVELY LISTEN FOR CHILDREN'S INTERESTS We listen to children and value their contributions. At our school, a major, schoolwide project started just this way. An area at the back of the playground had once been two tennis courts. However, the courts had fallen into major disrepair—cracked asphalt, uneven surfaces, overgrown vines covering a sagging twelve-foot chain-link fence, and rampant weeds taking over. Needless to say, the area was unusable for tennis or any other type of play. The children were not allowed to play in the area. During recess, a kindergarten child asked what the area was used for and Charlotte, in her best pondering role replied, "I'm not sure, what do you think it could be used for?" This generated much discussion among the children:

- "I think it could be a swimming pool. And we could jump off the side into the middle."
- "It could be a secret garden. We could go there and read where no one could see us."
- "We could make a racetrack and race go-carts there."

Charlotte replied, "I'm not sure. Maybe we could do some of those things. Which idea do you like the best?" The children surveyed the other kindergarten classes to see which idea they liked. The "secret garden" was the favored idea, but without a lot of money and support the staff knew that realistically, a "secret garden" was not possible. Much recess discussion centered on the area for the next few days, and the kindergarten children and teachers explored the area, imagining the possibilities. About the same time, a grant application came to the teachers' attention. They completed it, mailed it in, and were turned down. With resolve to complete the children's idea and to model perseverance for the children, the staff did not quit there. Local funding sources were successfully explored and an Outdoor Learning Environment was developed with a stream bed leading to wetland, woodland, prairie, and desert areas. The question from one kindergarten student grew into a schoolwide Applied Learning project. Figure 6–1 shows children working in the outdoor learning environment.

Decision Making

In general, we facilitate the decision-making discussion without actually deciding for the children. We consider how the choices are presented, making sure the

Figure 6–1. Students Working in the Outdoor Learning Environment

choices are acceptable. Because we accept the class's decision, we know that we do not have veto power after the fact. The decision-making opportunities are selected carefully, especially at the beginning of the year. Issues that are too complex can set the children up for failure (DeVries and Zan 1994).

Not all groups of young children can come easily to general agreement. We do not take a "telling role" with the students, but help them make a decision by reaching a general consensus or calling for a vote.

REACHING CONSENSUS As we lead children into making a decision, we may employ several strategies. We might give the children some background knowledge about the topics by reading aloud a book on each topic under consideration. A few children might conduct surveys to see if anyone in the class is interested in a particular topic. Then class meetings might be used to discuss how a majority of children can make a decision or how a person might give in to a decision to get something else in return. Negotiating and reaching a compromise are hard lessons for young children, but they are capable of learning these skills.

As the children involved in the Bat Display project returned from their trip to the zoo's exhibit, they expressed their ideas during a class meeting. Neesha's comment about making their display "like the part that we took the pictures of" was popular. That led to a lengthy give-and-take discussion of the class's ability (or inability) to create something "just like the zoo's display." As children work through multiple projects, they begin to find their own models for sharing what they have learned with others.

After the children identified five topics for the displays, Charlotte's quick sketch on large chart paper summarized the children's comments about what they planned to do. When she asked, "Is this what you are thinking about?" she was met with general agreement. While her summary of the children's comments restated them in a visual way, she did not "tell" the students how to make the displays.

VOTING   Voting is a process of self-regulation that helps children feel in control of what happens in their classroom. Over time and with experience, this group process transcends individual needs. Children learn, through the discussions, that sometimes what they want is not particularly good for the group, and their voting begins to reflect an "acceptance of majority rule and respect for minority views" (DeVries and Zan 1994, 160).

Young children like to vote. Sometimes they like to vote so much that they vote for all options. Many of them have not yet grasped the idea of choosing among alternatives and selecting just one. They want to vote for everything. One useful strategy we use is to ask the children to perform a specific action to indicate their vote. For example, "Those of you who want to vote for rocks, touch your knees while those of you who want to vote for pets, put your hands on your head." After a moment or two of indecisiveness, the children will indicate their preference and the votes can be counted.

RECORDING THE VOTE   While one person can be designated to count the votes, this may lead to miscounting or getting mixed up. We find other ways for young children to record their vote. Each vote can be recorded individually as the class is polled. A child can write tally marks on the board or place blocks under labeled sections of paper. Small sticky notes can be used to graph each child's vote. This is an opportunity to apply math skills in a real-world way.

From a First-Grade Teacher . . .

I use popsicle sticks with the children's names on them. When we need to vote on something, I grab the sticks and call on each child for their vote. I put the sticks into different piles depending on the child's answer. Then we count the sticks to see which option won.

During a Project: Beginning the Learning

Acquiring new knowledge is an important component of project work (Katz and Chard 2000), so, typically, this is where projects begin. In Applied Learning classes, a richness is added to the acquisition of new knowledge as children determine what they already know about the topic, search books, ask experts, and conduct observations.

Establishing a Knowledge Base

In general, after a topic is selected, the next step is for the teacher to read aloud one or two books that provide general information about the selected topic. Having some shared knowledge about the topic makes the class's planning go much easier. For one thing, young children often think they have become instant experts on any topic. As the Bat Display project was introduced, the first discussion centered on deciding if bats were birds. Various children offered their definite opinions about bats and were not swayed by the retorts of their peers. Justin challenged Charlotte's statement about bats, defending it with his background knowledge— "Yes they are, they fly!"—and Kelton supported his statement with evidence from a source respected by the class, *Stellaluna* by Janell Cannon (1993). However, as informative books were read aloud to the class, children began acquiring new facts. New information leads to new questions, which, in turn, leads to learning more information about the topic. With new knowledge flowing into the classroom, it becomes evident that ways to organize the information are needed.

Organizing Information

The process part of Applied Learning is important here. Once organizational strategies are learned, they can be applied to various content areas. The subject matter may change but the process of gathering, organizing, and learning new information is constant. While the product of a project is certainly important, we value the fact that children "learn how to learn" and develop the tools necessary to learn "anything about anything." An early childhood teacher will spend more class time teaching processes than a fourth- or fifth-grade teacher will. Children are also "learning metacognitive skills that allow them to transfer what they have learned to other learning situations" (Ward 1988, 46).

Without a textbook or other outside sources to predetermine what to do with information being gathered, you will need to teach organizational strategies. Because most young children are not accustomed to this type of inquiry, they do not bring much background knowledge about this process to the classroom. Even when they document only part of what they are learning, children end up with a large collection of notes, questions, answers, sketches, copied magazine articles, and a myriad of other pieces of paper. Young children do not know what to do with all this information, so we help children learn different ways to organize this information.

KWL CHARTS   One way to arrange the beginning research for a project with young children is to use a KWL chart (Ogle 1986; Glazer 1999). Children can write or draw for themselves, or they can dictate to the teacher what they know, their prior knowledge. These "known" facts are posted on the "K" part and the questions, or "What I Want to Know," are posted on the "W" part of the chart. In the Bat Display project, Charlotte recorded the list of "Bat Facts" on posterboard as the children dictated to her. As a project progresses, the KWL chart becomes a reference for the children. Information is added or deleted as the children confirm or challenge a fact. Additions are made to the "L" part of the chart as children acquire new knowledge, and fill in "What I Learned."

GRAPHIC ORGANIZERS   Many graphic organizers—KWL charts, Venn diagrams, T-charts, webs, compare/contrast charts—offer appropriate structures to help young children organize information. Using visual representations adds a structure to the knowledge so it can be more easily understood. Graphic organizers require students to maneuver information and grapple with what they do and do not know. They facilitate group work between students and teachers and among collaborative peers (Bromley, Irwin-DeVitis, and Modlo 1995). We use Venn diagrams to compare characteristics of two or three things. A simple T-chart with a large box at the top of the page, supported by smaller boxes under it, can be a help when teaching supporting details. A web diagram can be used to organize thoughts about a particular topic (Katz and Chard 2000).

INDIVIDUAL COLLECTIONS OF WORK   We also teach children how to organize their own work. Just as the KWL chart documents the group's inquiry, each student keeps individual documentation of what he or she has learned about the topic. Collections of drawings, writings, photographs of constructions, and/or photocopied information can be stored in individual pocket folders. This evidence does not magically fall into a child's folder. We teach this part of the process and support the children as they work over time to become organized. In Figure 6–2, Lisa is drawing a picture for her research folder.

Folders can be color-coded or labeled for easy access. For example, each committee member can have the same color pocket folder. We keep all the folders in a central place in the classroom, storing them so the children have access to them at anytime.

> **From a First-Grade Teacher . . .**
> The children were fascinated to see how many things they learned about Mexico during our study. I listed the facts they learned on the chart. They came up with the

Figure 6–2. Lisa Creating a Drawing for Her Research Folder

idea of color-coding the facts (like we do in Writers' Workshop) around the general topics—weather, clothes, food, and homes. They marked each fact with a different color, and we ended up cutting the chart apart and gluing similar facts together on another piece of tablet paper.

Individual composition books or notebooks can also be used to organize children's work. As a part of the Bat Display project, the children used bound composition books as "learning logs" to record factual details about bats. Among other things, they wrote definitions, used glue to attach photocopied maps of where bats live, and drew diagrams to show a bat's wingspan.

From a Kindergarten Teacher . . .
I started using project folders but with this class it just wasn't working. I finally decided to show the children how using sketch pads would help them keep all the work

in one place. I recruited some fifth graders to come help us, and we all sat down in the group space. We used glue sticks to glue all the stuff on different pages. This worked much better for this class. It dawned on me that I have to be willing to change something that's not working.

GROUP DATA   A large chart tablet (or posterboard) can be a project teacher's best friend. It serves as a visual reminder of children's responsibilities and a record of what has been accomplished. For example, it is helpful to organize committees by listing the children's names under their research areas. When this information is on a large chart tablet, everyone can use this list as a reminder of work to be done or as a guide for daily activity.

From a First-Grade Teacher . . .

I found it so helpful to use chart tablets to record the group's work. The decisions they made, the tallies of votes, the committee lists—everything was there in one place. I would see children flipping pages to find the information they needed. Recording on the tablet in front of the children also gives me another chance to model good literate practices for the children. I am always modeling how to sound out words or commenting about how to form a certain letter. Continuing this practice into project time seemed natural.

RECORDING RESEARCH   The research phase is when we teach strategies such as highlighting pertinent information, copying information to index cards (see Figure 6–3), and using self-stick notes to mark important parts of the text. Young children tend to overuse any new strategy. They often end up with long passages of highlighted text or notes flagging every page in a book. It takes practice—and teaching and reteaching by the teacher—for young children to learn to evaluate the merits of different passages.

Information that a child wants from a book can be photocopied. Children flag the page they want copied with an initialed self-stick note. An adult—or older student—can copy the page and return it to the child. Then the child can highlight or use this information as he or she wants.

Large index cards work well for noting relevant information or writing questions. They are easily handled by young children and offer a limited space for writing. Writing in this small space often reassures the child who sees filling a whole page as overwhelming. Index cards also work well for recording captions for photographs, drawings, or label copy for displays.

Figure 6–3. Children Recording Research on Index Cards

Consulting Multiple Resources

In Applied Learning projects, it is not sufficient to access only one source of information. Children need to locate information in a variety of forms. As children search for answers to the questions they raised, we encourage them to find printed resources, interview experts, and, depending on the topic, make personal observations. While the research typically begins with reading books, it is then expanded to other resources—various printed materials, experts, and observations.

Initially, the topic of the project drives the research. Then, when the end product is selected, research often takes a turn toward an investigation of how adults produce that particular product. For example, after researching a topic and deciding to make an exhibit, children would visit a museum to learn how the museum staff develops exhibits. Children who read about and observed gerbils might decide to write a manual about the care and feeding of a gerbil. They would seek out the advice of someone who writes manuals.

Each project offers the opportunity to learn about different resources. In the Hurricane Video project, children consulted books from the school library, the public library, and several bookstores; watched weather and hurricane reports on cable weather stations; and browsed newspapers, magazines, and encyclopedias.

They wrote letters and emails to people they knew who had been in hurricanes, and called several of those people. Although two of the students suggested that we all "fly to Florida so we could see some real hurricanes," the closest the children came to hurricane observation was watching informational videos. In the Bat Display project, information came from library books, books contributed by the families, downloaded Internet information, CD-ROM encyclopedias, magazine articles, and a field trip to the zoo's temporary exhibit about bats.

PRINTED RESOURCES   Books are perhaps the easiest to access in a school setting. Expository texts are quite appealing to young children. They delight in the discovery of factual information. However, most school libraries have limited resources, so the search for books normally extends beyond the school. Families often take children to public libraries or to a local bookstore. Even with emerging reading skills, young children learn rather quickly how to gain information from photographs and drawings, decode key words in captions, or mark passages they would like read to them. We explore such options as having older students in the school or adult volunteers come into the class to read aloud portions of the text.

We do not want children to form the idea that books contain the "best" information. Because expository information quickly gets out of date, children need to know that there are other resources—newspapers, magazines, brochures, pamphlets, and newsletters—that make current information available. Internet searches supply any number of websites to locate information. We schedule Internet search times when adult volunteers can work with students. This supervision avoids the issue of accidentally accessing less than desirable websites. Adults can also help children understand that anyone can post anything to the Internet, and that not everything is necessarily correct. We encourage children to consult many kinds of resources during the research component of a project.

EXPERTS   It is not always necessary to find a printed source for information the children are seeking. Frequently, the easiest, fastest way to find the answer to a question is to ask just the right person. "Experts" can be invited to the classroom to share their expertise, or the children can visit, write, email, or call the expert. The entire class does not have to be involved in each contact. One child or group of children can report the findings to the class. Before young children contact experts to ask questions, we teach specific lessons about interviewing techniques and hold quite a few practice sessions before their first interview.

When working with young children, it is important to remember that an expert does not have to be an adult who works in a professional field. Anyone can be an expert—an aunt who loves to garden, a grandmother who is accomplished at creating computer drawings, or a father who builds furniture as a hobby. Each could serve as an expert to the class for different parts of different projects.

An expert does not even have to be an adult. A child in another class who has raised hamsters for two years is an expert in that field. A child who lived in Mexico City for a year can be consulted about the customs he observed in that city. A child who took art lessons at the local museum can give advice about mixing colors to create a display or exhibit. Older children often serve as experts for younger children. The school's "News Crew" modeled how to make good announcements over the school's public address system for the kindergarten children during the Bat Display project.

From a Kindergarten Teacher . . .
When my kindergarten children were in the midst of the project to beautify the appearance of the side entrance to our school, they needed to decide what plants would grow in concrete urns. I wondered aloud, "What plants should we put in the pots? Hum-m-m . . . who knows a lot about plants?" The children were quick to respond, "Judy! She helps the big kids work in the flower beds on Friday. Maybe she would help." Judy, mother of classmate Gwen, was contacted and shared her advice with the class. Of course, I knew that Judy was an active parent volunteer in the school and had already checked with her to see if she would come into the classroom to advise the children. This "behind the scenes" preparation pays off in success for the children.

OBSERVATIONS   Observations are another source of information. Some topics lend themselves to observation in classrooms or in the outdoor environment near the school. If the project is related to animals, children observe pets in their own or other classrooms. If the children are investigating growing things, they observe the flower bed outside their classroom window and/or the vegetable garden planted at the back of the playground. Gracie's class's observations of temperature changes led to the establishment of a school weather station, with daily weather reports posted in the hall.

Other topics are not so easily observed in the school environment. Field trips are often required to give the children firsthand observation of and experience with the topic. If a project relates to wild animals, children need the experience of observing animals in a zoo or a wildlife preserve. If the project is to research playground equipment so they can make recommendations to the principal about the outdoor budget expenditures, the children need to explore several local playgrounds. If writing a play is a component of a project, then the children need to attend a local professional performance.

In Applied Learning classrooms, a field trip is not just the opportunity to get out of the school to see something unique. Before going on the field trip, we outline the research expectations as we help the children determine what will be observed and how the information will be remembered and used. We teach the children several ways to document what they observe. They can:

- Take sketch pads and markers with them in backpacks
- Get clipboards, paper, and pencils from an adult at a meeting time during the field trip
- Use hand-held tape recorders
- Take photographs

In Figure 6–4, we see children sketching their observations during a field trip.

From a First-Grade Teacher . . .
My first graders had the idea to make an alphabet book of zoo animals as part of our animal project. We started searching books to find a zoo animal to match every letter in the alphabet, but then the idea came up of taking photographs of animals from our local zoo and putting those into a book. So we went to the zoo, armed with cameras and poster-sized replicas of every letter of the alphabet. What a great time the kids had, posing with the giant G by the giraffes, with the W by the white tiger, etc.! On the way back to school, one of the parents had our film developed at one of those one hour developing places. How great to have the photographs developed and back in the classroom the same day!

Firsthand experiences are almost always superior to watching videotapes or hearing a report of a face-to-face interview. In the Bat Display project, the children could have created their displays without the field trip to the zoo. They read enough books, websites, encyclopedias, and magazine articles to learn facts about bats, but observing the bats in the zoo made the experience much richer for the children.

As the children consult multiple sources of information to answer the questions they have raised, they need the teacher's guidance. We constantly monitor and observe the children as they work.

Monitoring the Work

We observe the children's work very carefully and note knowledge the children are gaining and the skills they are using. We also observe children's behaviors as they work alone or in small groups for insight into their feelings about their work and dispositions to use what they are learning. We eavesdrop on conversations,

Figure 6–4. On a Field Trip, Sketching Observations

constantly scan the overall classroom, and evaluate each child's progress. Monitoring the work and planning specific lessons for individuals or small groups is a major part of the teacher's role as a project continues. Chapter 8 has an additional discussion of evaluation methods.

During the first-grade class's study of reptiles, Deborah acted as a conscientious, proactive observer. During project work, she moved around the room, stopping to chat with each committee about their task(s) for the day. After she was convinced that all children were engaged in their work, she carried out plans made from her notes during the previous day's project time. She called together a group of five students for a short reminder lesson about using periods in their writing. She talked with three students about including more detail in their drawings. She read part of a web page to a committee who had searched the Internet and downloaded information the day before. She found the committee who was creating its own reptile alphabet book and taught the students how to use an index to find the letters they were missing. Her plans were interrupted when two boys started arguing loudly. She quietly helped them solve their disagreement, then redirected their behavior back to their plan for project work.

From a First-Grade Teacher . . .
My instruction tends to be more on target during project work. As I watch the children to see what they need, I teach skills when the child needs them. I had taught capitalizing the first letter of words in a title. But many of the children didn't do it until they were copying the titles of the books they were using in their research. I showed them again, and they put the skill to use.

Documenting Children's Work

The very nature of project work allows us to support children where they are, teaching skills, providing a specific bit of knowledge, or talking about how they feel about their work. This scaffolding of children's learning is probably the most effective teaching strategy the teacher uses all day because it is so focused on what individual children need (Bodrova and Leong 1996). In order to keep records of the progress of each child, we use some form of anecdotal record keeping. Sometimes it is as simple as a tabbed loose-leaf notebook, with a section for each child. Or the system may be as intricate as keeping individual files on the teacher's laptop computer. However it is done, this documentation is the heart of charting children's progress (Helm, Beneke, and Steinheimer 1997). It is from these observations that you plan the next step in each child's learning. More specific information about assessment of project work can be found in Chapter 8.

Completing a Project

At some point in the research process, the concept of sharing the learning with other people will come up. Young children often believe that other people are as interested in their learning as they are, so sometimes children bring up the idea of sharing what they know. Charlotte's kindergarten class studied bats and create displays because Charlotte knew the entire school was going to be invited to visit the zoo's temporary exhibit on bats. As soon as her class found out that all classes would tour the zoo's exhibit, the kindergarten children decided that they knew more about bats than any other class. They believed they had to share what they had learned about bats. Comments from Kyle—"We need to tell the fifth graders about Dr. Merlin Tuttle"—and Demond—"My brother said his class is going to the zoo, too. But he doesn't know anything about bats"—led to sharing information about bats on the school's public address system. In another project, first-grade students were concerned that "little kindergartners might be scared of hurricanes and can't read about them as good as us" and wanted to alleviate those

Figure 6–5. Bat Display Poster

fears in some way. Both conversations led to real-world products—a hall display about bats (see Figure 6–5) and an informational videotape about hurricanes.

Deciding on a Project's End Product

The children did not come to these decisions on their own. Once again, our wonderings and informal musings prodded the project's developments. Quietly asking Demond, "Does your brother understand this stuff as well as you do?" meets two objectives. First, it encourages and recognizes the child (Cameron et al. 1997). The question clearly recognizes Demond's progress and plants a seed in his mind that he might know something that his older brother might not understand. Second, the question unobtrusively molds the project and moves it along.

Another way that end products are determined is to let the children brainstorm possible outcomes. A second-grade class wanted to conduct a survey to find out the birthdays of everyone in the school and honor everyone's birthday. As they began to brainstorm birthday celebrations, the first idea was to hold a birthday party for each child. As that idea was explored, the children realized that they could not provide a birthday cake and decorations for all 378 children in the school. They finally settled on making birthday cards for each child. The children considered all the ideas, listed pros and cons, and supported their opinions. Dialogue and group interaction, coupled with logic and reasoning skills, make for powerful learning.

Examining Models

Once the product of a project is determined, then we begin to look for competent models of what that product might look like. First-grade children who wanted to videotape themselves reading stories to younger children viewed episodes from the PBS series *Reading Rainbow* to determine how the reader held the book, paused for effect, and kept the interest of the viewer. The children involved in the Bat Display project wanted to make announcements on the school's public address system and contacted the fourth- and fifth-grade students for tips. They knew these older students made the daily announcements on the speaker and considered them "experts."

Competent models of print materials are easily found. Advertisements are printed in the local paper, brochures are available in most retail establishments, signs are posted on the street, etc. Good project-based teachers are constantly on the lookout for suitable competent models.

Presenting a Finished Product

Our role in sharing a completed product is, as always, to step back and let the children have center stage. This is not to say that we do not assist the children in polishing these final steps, but our role is one of support and guidance. For example, in opening their rock and fossil exhibit, "the kindergarten children played multiple roles as they greeted visitors, passed out exhibit brochures and refreshments, and explained the exhibit" (Diffily 1996, 74).

After the presentation, the teacher and children together evaluate the project. Self-assessments and group assessments are discussed and completed. They return to the knowledge the children had before the project began—the KWL chart, the list of dictated facts, or the children's learning logs. Frequently children are amazed by the amount of knowledge they have gained during a project. As five-year-old Logan said, "I never knew I knew so much!" This "knowing" sense of accomplishment sets the stage for the next project to begin.

Reinforcing Newly Gained Knowledge

Just as the teacher leads a group evaluation of the project, he or she also spends some private time reflecting on the project's strengths and weaknesses. In any learning experience, there are areas that could be improved, and projects are no different. As they reflect about decisions they made during the project, teachers may find that they were too directive with children or that they waited too long to intervene in a situation where children had difficulty reaching consensus. When considering teacher/student interactions, teachers may decide to work more with students on respectful language or in sharing responsibility for different tasks within the project. A teacher may discover that a piece of the curriculum was missing, for example, the difficulty the children had with writing letters was because the children were not familiar enough with the letter writing format. By recognizing these strengths and weaknesses, the teacher can adjust plans for the next project and make the learning appropriate for the children's needs.

The project is over. Some tasks that seemed important at the time were lost along the way. Other work took their place. Successes were celebrated; failures learned from. The teacher taught—as a facilitator, mentor, model, and ponderer—and the children learned—more than they thought they would or could.

Sometimes the completion of one project leads directly to the next project—beautifying the side entrance to the school caused the children to notice the overgrown flower bed outside the classroom window. Then other times, the learning of one project highlights the next needed piece of curriculum—searching for a way to improve their reading habits led first-grade children to the production of the *Reading Rainbow*–like videos.

We approach learning and teaching in a new way. Teachers still teach and children still learn. But the children are learning and the teachers are teaching skills that will be used throughout the students' lifetimes to help them be "responsible, sociable, self-managing, and resourceful adults" (U.S. Department of Labor 1992, 42).

Summary

As an Applied Learning teacher begins a first project, he or she gathers ideas from children's interests or curriculum topics. The teacher's role of model and mentor is different from the traditional role of imparting knowledge. He or she teaches decision-making strategies and organizational techniques. Teachers support children as they begin a project, access and organize multiple sources of information, and create an end product.

7

Learning Skills Through Projects

The test of understanding involves neither repetition of information learned nor performance of practices mastered. Rather it involves the appropriate application of concepts and principles to questions or problems that are newly posed.
—HOWARD GARDNER 1993

Our competitive world requires that our students learn extensive knowledge and skills in the academic content areas. Beyond that, they need to apply what they learn in the content areas in multiple situations. We believe that Applied Learning projects are powerful tools that enable us to embed skills while ensuring the educational outcomes of lifelong learning and enhanced personal qualities. Not only do we teach important academic skills, we also include other skills and personal qualities that are essential to functioning successfully in the world. These essential skills include critical thinking, interpersonal, communication, and technological skills. Like other teachers who are concerned with the global outcomes of education, we believe:

> It is not enough that (students) become broadly and deeply knowledgeable, and academically and technically skilled. This is an all-important goal of education. But it is not enough. Children must also become interpersonally sensitive and adept. They must learn to understand and effectively manage their emotions and their personal needs and desires. And they must become deeply committed to values of justice and caring. A humane and decent democracy requires a citizenry that cares deeply about the common good, is thoughtful in word and deed, and is committed to living ethically (Schaps 1998, 1).

Embedding Skills

A vital characteristic of Applied Learning is that skills are embedded into the tasks that constitute projects. First, all projects address many academic skills—adequate reading skills are needed as children read texts to find answers to their questions; writing skills are taught as children record their thoughts; math concepts are introduced and taught when children need to count things, measure something, or collect and graph data; and science and social studies concepts are presented as children explore real-world topics. If skills were not an integral part of a project, there would be no reason for children to engage in project work.

Second, we teach skills as they are needed. The "teachable moment" (Vygotsky 1962) comes up often in project work. Many teachable moments occurred throughout the projects discussed in previous chapters. For example, in the Posters About Mexico project, Susan taught interviewing techniques before college students from Mexico visited the classroom. In the Reptile Exhibit project, Deborah taught first-grade students how to use an index so they could complete their reptile alphabet books. While state standards did not specifically require these skills to be taught at these grade levels, we recognized these as teachable moments. We knew that children needed these skills to accomplish what they had planned or were already working on, so we taught the needed skills.

Third, we constantly observe what children are doing during project time and identify additional skills that we can "work into" the tasks of project work. If we cannot find ways to mesh skills with what the children choose, we lead children into choosing tasks that include the required skills.

From a Second-Grade Teacher . . .

I often think about a statement made during a workshop I attended about Applied Learning. One of the presenters said, "You don't wait for a bluebird to land on your window to study birds." It sounds a bit silly out of context, but it reminds me of a really important concept. We do not have to wait for the teachable moment to teach something that children need to learn. If state or district mandates say students are expected to "use diagrams, charts, or illustrations as appropriate to the text" (that's a second-grade writing standard in my state) then as the teacher you have to teach that skill. Maybe you can incorporate that into a project and maybe you can't. You still have to teach that skill, and if you believe in Applied Learning, you figure out ways to offer children opportunities to use that skill in several real-world kinds of ways. This sounds hard to do, but when you start thinking in this manner, it becomes second nature to you to always be looking for ways to teach needed skills.

Academic Skills

Applying learned skills in authentic situations is the primary focus of Applied Learning projects. Children learn and apply skills within projects at almost the same time. We accept each child's attempt at using the skill that was taught. While some children pick up the skill almost immediately, other children struggle to apply what they can verbalize, and other children are not yet ready to learn that particular skill at that time. We acknowledge that a range of ability is acceptable. We know that in subsequent projects, we will reteach a skill as children need it to complete a part of another project. In reviewing young children's work in Applied Learning classrooms, it is clearly evident that the application of skills, not the mastery of skills, is valued most highly. Skills from all content areas are embedded in the work of projects.

From a First-Grade Teacher . . .
As I helped my first semester first graders publish their reports for the exhibit about the ocean, I despaired over the unevenness of the quality of the work. I had asked the children to record six facts about their topic. Then I showed them how to add a beginning that would "catch the reader's interest," organize the six facts into logical order, and sum up the report with a conclusion. About a third of the class did a great job, but they were my top readers. The low readers didn't even have six facts recorded. Then I realized this was their first attempt at writing nonfiction reports and they would have opportunities to write in this genre again. After that I could relax and help each individual child do the best he or she could, instead of expecting everyone to meet the highest standard.

An example of the six recorded facts is shown in Figure 7–1.

Reading

Most people agree that of all the academic skills required of elementary school children, learning to read is the most important. In reality, reading is not a skill, but a series of very complex skills. Children rarely learn to read as the result of a single type of instruction. Most children need to be involved in a variety of literacy experiences to develop into competent readers. The National Association for the Education of Young Children suggests that young children need:

- daily experiences of being read to and independently reading meaningful and engaging stories and informational texts;
- a balanced instructional program that includes systematic code instruction along with meaningful reading and writing activities;

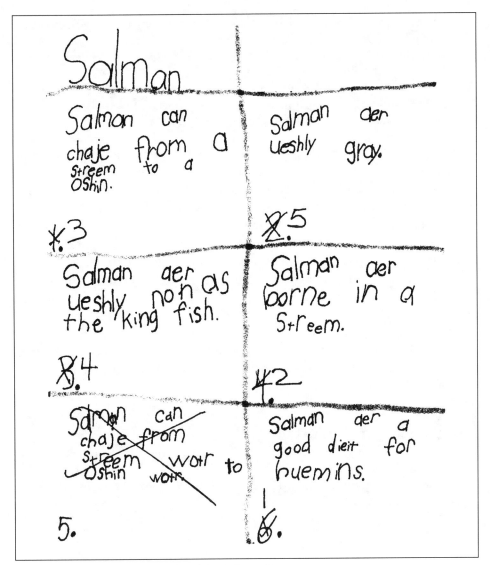

Figure 7–1. Sentences Reordered for Salmon Report

- daily opportunities and teacher support to write many kinds of texts for different purposes, including stories, lists, messages to others, poems, reports, and responses to literature;
- writing experiences that allow the flexibility to use nonconventional forms of writing at first (invented or phonic spelling) and over time move to conventional forms;

- opportunities to work in small groups for focused instruction and collaboration with other children;
- an intellectually engaging and challenging curriculum that expands knowledge of the world and vocabulary, and
- adaptation of instructional strategies or more individualized instruction if the child fails to make expected progress in reading or when literacy skills are advanced (Neuman, Copple, and Bredekamp 2000, 16–17).

During Applied Learning projects, we provide all of these literacy experiences for all students. We read to children during every project time. From listening to informational texts, children learn facts about the project's topic. They also learn reading strategies we teach to the whole class. As they conduct research and document their learning, we work with individuals or small groups on reading strategies and writing skills at individual targeted skill levels. Projects offer children opportunities to write different kinds of texts, some in draft form and others that require students to work through all of the writing stages to produce a final piece. Throughout projects, children work in small groups with the teacher's support and guidance. The flexible structure of Applied Learning projects lends itself to differentiating instruction for the children. We can modify content, process, or product based on what we know about each student (Tomlinson 1999). This flexible structure allows the teacher to enrich a gifted child's experience while reinforcing concepts with a struggling child.

From a Kindergarten Teacher . . .

The children were doing research for a project related to the solar system. Nicholas was sitting on the floor reading about Saturn when a parent came in to help read "hard words." The parent stopped and listened to Nicholas. Amazed, she commented, "Nicholas, I didn't know you could read so well." Nicholas gave one of those are-you-crazy looks that kindergarten children do so well and responded, "I'm not reading, I'm doing research."

Writing

Children write for a variety of reasons and direct their writing to a variety of audiences within each project. And, just as we embed and extend reading skills into project work, we also embed and extend writing skills into the same projects.

In the Posters About Mexico project, children used writing skills in many different ways. They wrote fiction stories about Mexican children, documented questions they had and answers they found, and added words to their personal dictionaries. They crafted letters and email messages asking for information from people who had visited Mexico. They wrote fact cards about what they were learning and used them in the posters they created.

The act of teaching takes different approaches during each project. At times, we might decide that a lesson is appropriate for the entire class. For example, when children begin to write research questions on index cards, direct instruction about writing questions is appropriate. We discuss what a question is, how it ends with a question mark, how to fit the question on the card, and why spacing is important. We model how to write a question and use interactive writing strategies (McCarrier, Pinnell, and Fountas 1999). At other times, we might work with small groups or individual students on writing skills when our evaluations indicate additional instruction is needed. These approaches to teaching writing are compatible with the Standards for the English Language Arts as written by the National Council of Teachers of English and the International Reading Association (NCTE/IRA 1996).

Projects offer many opportunities to teach embedded skills, take advantage of the "teachable moment" as the need for a particular skill arises, and expand project work to include other necessary skills.

Mathematics

The National Council of Teachers of Mathematics (2000) states that mathematics is more than a collection of skills to be mastered. Mathematics includes investigation, reasoning, communication, and context. This practical approach of learning math is utilized during Applied Learning projects. Students are actively involved in authentic mathematical experiences. Best practices for teaching mathematics (Zemelman, Daniels, and Hyde 1998) are used during projects as students apply mathematical concepts to accomplish tasks related to the project.

Most Applied Learning projects provide opportunities to:

- Count objects
- Use basic addition and subtraction facts
- Collect data
- Make graphs, surveys, and budgets
- Display data
- Make statements and predictions
- Draw conclusions based on information
- Estimate numerically and spatially
- Compare quantities
- Measure
- Use money
- Tell time

Each Applied Learning project lends itself to different math skills, but several activities are common to most projects. For example, children often count the facts that they have recorded and compare quantities. They use time-telling skills to keep track of the amount of time they have for their committee work. They send notes home to families about different parts of the project and track responses that have been returned to school. They also use one-to-one correspondence to determine the number of invitations needed to send to individuals or classes within the school to celebrate the completion of the project's end product, and they track those responses as well.

While we capitalize on the "teachable moment" to reinforce skills, we also expand project work to include necessary math skills or design specific projects (or pre-project experiences) to cover specific math skills.

Science

Science concepts lend themselves well to the research-based nature of projects. They are frequently selected as the topic for Applied Learning projects, and because projects support child-directed research, they meet national standards.

The National Science Education Standards describe science "as an active process. Learning science is something that students do, not something that is done to them. 'Hands-on' activities, while essential, are not enough. Students must have 'minds-on' experiences as well" (National Research Council 1995, 2). Applied Learning projects offer many different opportunities to apply science knowledge and fine-tune science skills.

Among some of the state science standards the children met while working on the Rocks and Fossils Exhibit project are:

- ask questions about organisms, objects, and events,
- gather information using simple equipment and tools to extend the senses,
- identify and use senses as tools of observation,
- make observations using tools including hand lenses, balances, cups, bowls, and computers,
- sort organisms and objects into groups according to their parts and describe how the groups are formed,
- identify a particular organism or object as living or nonliving,
- identify ways that the Earth can provide resources for life,
- observe and describe properties of rocks, soil, and water. (Texas Education Agency 1998)

In addition to meeting multiple science standards, the children's project work for the Rock and Fossil Museum met many of social studies standards, such as:

- identify and describe the physical characteristics of places such as landforms, bodies of water, natural resources, and weather;
- obtain information about a topic using a variety of oral sources such as conversations, interviews, and music;
- sequence and categorize information;
- create visual and written material including pictures, maps, timelines, and graphs.
- use a problem-solving process to identify a problem, gather information, list and consider options, consider advantages and disadvantages, choose and implement a solution, and evaluate the effectiveness of the solution. (TEA 1998)

Social Studies

A framework offered by the National Council for the Social Studies leans heavily toward the constructivist approach to teaching and learning. Of the ten "characteristics" suggested by the framework, seven focus on the process of learning and the integration of all curriculum areas into broad social studies themes. This view of teaching social studies is quite compatible with Applied Learning projects.

Children who created the Posters About Mexico learned significant information about Mexico: its people, how they live, where they live, what kinds of foods are preferred, how they dress, and what kinds of traditions they celebrate. This project met all of the social studies characteristics described by the National Council for the Social Studies. Because the project was based on a social studies topic, it is natural that children learned many social studies concepts and specific facts about Mexico.

Among some of the social studies state standards the children met while working on the Posters About Mexico project are:

- use vocabulary related to time and chronology, including before, after, next, first, and last,
- identify the physical characteristics of places such as landforms, bodies of water, natural resources, and weather,
- identify the human characteristics of places such as types of houses and ways of earning a living,
- identify basic human needs,
- explain how basic human needs of food, clothing, and shelter can be met,
- identify personal attributes common to all people such as physical characteristics,
- identify differences among people,
- obtain information about a topic using a variety of oral sources such as conversations, interviews, and music,
- identify main ideas from oral, visual, and print sources,
- express ideas orally based on knowledge and experiences,
- create and interpret visuals including pictures and maps,

- use a problem-solving process to identify a problem, gather information, list and consider options, consider advantages and disadvantages, choose and implement a solution, and evaluate the effectiveness of the solution,
- use a decision-making process to identify a situation that requires a decision, gather information, identify options, predict consequences, and take action to implement a decision, and
- explain the use of voting as a method for group decision making. (TEA 1998)

Just like science-related projects can help children meet social studies standards, science processes and concepts can be integrated into projects that have a social studies topic. In the Posters About Mexico project, children met the following science standards:

- learned how to use and conserve resources and materials;
- made decisions using information;
- discussed and justified the merits of decisions;
- recorded and compared collected information;
- measured organisms and objects and parts of organisms and objects, using non-standard units such as paper clips, hands, and pencils;
- observed and described the parts of plants;
- observed and recorded changes in the life cycle of organisms;
- identified and described a variety of natural sources of water including streams, lakes, and oceans (TEA 1998).

Just as basic academic skills of reading, writing, mathematics, science, and social studies are important in projects, we equally value the thinking skills that are taught within project work.

Thinking Skills

As important as academic skills are, they are not sufficient to make adults effective in the workplace or young children successful in Applied Learning classrooms. Thinking skills that transcend the learning and applying of basic academic skills are necessary. These thinking skills include creative thinking, problem solving, decision making, reasoning, and learning how to learn (U.S. Department of Labor 1991). Applied Learning projects offer multiple opportunities for children to learn, utilize, and enhance these thinking skills.

Creative Thinking

Creative thinking requires children to generate new ideas or look at something in a new, fresh way. Imagination is freely used while connections are made. New possibilities are explored as we encourage children to "think outside the box." In the

Math Games project, second-grade children looked at something quite common, board games, in a new way. Game boards the children created for Math-O-Ween demonstrated their creative thinking. Putting the game board on the floor and having the participants be the human game pieces is definitely a new way of looking at game boards. Creative thinking such as this leads to problem solving.

Problem Solving

Learning to solve problems while considering all the factors related to the problem is an important step for young children. They recognize problems and usually come up with an answer to the problem. At times, this solution is not best for the whole group or project; just best for the child suggesting the solution. For example, when a second-grade class was discussing the problem of how to honor all the birthdays in the school, John suggested creating a Birthday Museum as a way to celebrate birthdays. He had been in a K–1 class that created several museum exhibits. He enjoyed his positive experiences related to creating exhibits, so his answer for every end product was "let's make a museum." His solution in this case was not appropriate. He was suggesting a solution that he wanted, not considering the logistics or practicality of the suggestion. As the class reasoned through his suggestion and tried to visualize what a Birthday Museum would include, he understood and withdrew his suggestion.

In this case, the conversation that followed John's suggestion was an important part of that activity. The other children did not reject his suggestion outright. They just asked questions until John realized that a birthday museum would not be a wise way to celebrate all the birthdays in the school. It is through these discussions that children learn that some solutions to problems are better than others. Quite often, children lead other children in developing certain thinking skills.

Decision Making

Decision-making skills are closely related to problem-solving skills. We provide children with opportunities to make many decisions during the course of an Applied Learning project. Some of their decisions are as simple as whether to use markers or colored pencils for a sign they are creating. But most decisions are not quite as neutral as choosing between two media. Decisions common to most projects include selecting partners or committee members, picking a committee to serve on, designating tasks to specific committee members, organizing information, choosing topics and an end product. We teach children to generate alternatives, then choose the best option. Practice in choosing the best alternative is an important part of developing thinking skills and, certainly, a part of most Applied Learning projects.

Reasoning

The ability to choose among alternatives is related to the development of reasoning skills. We teach children to consider factors related to the options, evaluate the pros and cons of different alternatives, and choose one option through the process of reasoning. The second graders used reasoning skills to determine the type of math game they would create. Each group examined the options they had brainstormed, discussed how much math they could put into each game idea they had, made notes about materials they would need, and talked about the types of people who might enjoy each game idea. Then they used their developing reasoning skills to consider all that information and make a final choice.

Learning How to Learn

The skill of "learning how to learn" is perhaps most directly supported by project work. Children who work through multiple Applied Learning projects can use the processes and skills learned through projects and learn virtually anything they want to learn. Children who have formulated questions—about Mexico, hurricanes, bats, rocks and fossils, and mathematics—can do the same for any other topic. Children who have created museum exhibits, informational videos, hallway displays, and their own games can share their knowledge with others in multiple ways. Planning and implementing Applied Learning projects provides the knowledge and experience to learn about any topic that interests the children.

Over an entire school year, children become quite accomplished at applying thinking skills, especially considering their young age. They become quite good at generating new ideas as they work through projects. They learn different ways to approach problems, frequently relying on brainstorming possible options and choosing the option with the strongest rationale. They make decisions and use reasoning skills to make those decisions. Children are challenged in every project to enhance thinking skills as they also learn interpersonal skills.

Interpersonal Skills

People, adults or children, who are adept at academic and thinking skills also need other skills to be successful. They need to get along with the people with whom they work. Both schools and the workplace require that individuals work alone and in groups. Part of this "getting along" is based on interpersonal skills, or interpersonal intelligence.

Howard Gardner (1993) discusses interpersonal intelligence as the "core capacity to notice distinctions in others, in particular, contrasts in their moods, temperaments, motivations, and intentions" (23), and to use this information about other people to facilitate working together. This sounds like a very sophisticated skill to expect of young children, yet we find evidence of interpersonal skills virtually every time that young children work on projects.

Children in Applied Learning classrooms certainly have a myriad of opportunities to use these skills. The nature of project-based learning requires that children work in differently configured groups every day. Over time, they learn how to "read" their peers. If one child is having a bad day, the other children in the group recognize that and interact with that child differently, not expecting the same level of work as they normally would. When two children in a committee have a disagreement, the entire group helps resolve the problem so that the work can continue. These small-group interactions not only increase children's interpersonal skills, they also enhance communication skills.

Communication Skills

Communicating effectively is central to success in school, as well as in life. This includes communicating orally and in writing. Every child enters school with different abilities. Some children easily talk with adults or peers. Other children struggle to communicate with anyone outside their own families. Some children find expressing their thoughts in writing as natural as communicating orally. For other children, written communication requires great effort. Wherever children are on the continuum of communication skills, teachers need to discover their strengths and build on them.

Being a good listener is a part of effective communication. Gemmet (1977) described a good listener as one who does not interrupt, does not judge, thinks before answering, faces the speaker, is close enough to hear, watches nonverbal behavior, is aware of biases, concentrates on what is being said, avoids rehearsing answers while another person is talking, and does not insist on having the last word. Anyone who has worked with young children knows that these skills are not naturally acquired. Applied Learning teachers make listening skills apparent to children. We model these skills, describe them in detail, and help the children practice them. Because Applied Learning projects require that children work in large groups and in multiple small groups, there are many opportunities for children to practice these skills. Effective communicators develop over time as we make the elements of good listening clear to children during class meetings and as we reinforce them while children work together.

From a Kindergarten Teacher . . .
Because we had so many visitors to our school, the staff made the decision that, in most cases, teachers would not interact with the visitors during class time. The chil-

dren would do that. Each class chose docents and brainstormed what to say to class-room visitors. All the docents developed their own style and practiced how they would approach the visitors and what they would say about the class. Most adults were very impressed with the sophistication of the children acting as docents. You can imagine my surprise one afternoon when I heard one of the children say, "Well, are you going to stand there and watch, or are you going to come in and learn something?" I was even more surprised when I looked up and saw a very powerful man standing in the doorway. He was chairman of the Democratic Party of a large urban city and on the school board there. He smiled and stepped into the classroom. He stayed for more than half an hour asking questions and politely listening to the do-cent's answers. The minute he left the room, I met the docent at the door to have a chat about better ways to invite visitors into our class.

As children prepare for life in the real world by learning academic skills and fine-tuning their thinking skills and interpersonal and communication skills, they must also learn skills of the twenty-first century. Technological skills are taught during projects and are an integral part of the children's work.

Technological Skills

In Applied Learning classrooms, technology is never an add-on to the curriculum. It is an integral part of the children's work. "The mere presence of computers guarantees nothing about . . . education" (Healy 1998, 67), but when technology is presented as a way of learning and accomplishing tasks, it can support children's social interaction (Clements 1998), motivation (Elkind 1998), and collaboration.

We teach children to use technology as it is needed to accomplish something, or if it makes doing something easier. For example, during most projects, children produce many different kinds of written material. They write business letters and emails, finalize reports, create signs and label copy, produce brochures, and more. If young children were required to write all these items by hand with exact letter-ing so that other people could easily read their writing, it would take an inordinate amount of time. When children key in their draft ideas, they can easily edit and revise their work and change wording, font, style, and size with ease.

> When exploration of a concept encourages students to write letters, stories, poems, or reports, using a word processor allows children to compose, revise, add, and re-move text without being distracted by the fine motor aspects and tedium of forming letters (Davis and Shade 1994, 1).

Word processing, with its accompanying spell check, thesaurus, and grammar check, is available to most students in kindergarten, first, and second grades. With age-appropriate instruction, young children quickly learn to use these as tools for producing project work. Other forms of technology are also used as an integral part of project-based learning. Young children learn to use the telephone, fax machines, databases, spreadsheets, laser discs, CD-ROMs, scanners, and digital cameras as they see how this equipment supports their work. While not all Applied Learning classrooms have equal access to technology, we help students incorporate the available technology into their project work.

In the Reptile Museum project, children used what they had learned about technology within their project work. They searched the Internet to find answers to some of their questions. They also emailed questions to relatives or friends of their families who knew something about reptiles. Members of a committee gathered around the computer exploring different fonts and sizes for text. They used word processing programs and spell check while creating final "facts" to be posted in the museum. They created signs and label copy with word processing and drawing and stamping software programs. None of these tools were complicated to learn. They were learning how technology can be used to "do what they need to do."

Through day-to-day use of technology, children learn to understand the role of technology in "collecting, storing, retrieving, and dealing with information as well as in transmitting it" (American Association for the Advancement of Science 1993, 200). Technology in Applied Learning classrooms is not used just for the sake of using technology. It is always used as a tool to accomplish work related to projects.

All of these skills are addressed in one way or another through project work. Most academic skill requirements of reading, writing, mathematics, science, and social studies can be embedded into projects. Additionally, thinking, interpersonal, communication, and technological skills are taught during project time.

Summary

Schools are concerned with preparing young people for their place in the world—their job, family, and community. Whether a citizen works in a blue- or white-collar occupation, he or she must possess a fundamental knowledge of academic skills and must have good thinking, interpersonal, communication, and technological skills. Applied Learning embeds academic skills within project work and ensures that personal qualities are fostered. While this is a different approach to schooling, it is one that empowers children and leads to a lifelong desire to learn.

8

Assessing Children's Work
and Progress

Assessment is the process of gathering information about children in order to make decisions about their education. Teachers obtain useful information about children's knowledge, skills, and progress by observing, documenting, and reviewing children's work over time.

—Toni S. Bickart, Judy R. Jablon, and Diane Trister Dodge 1999

Purposes of Assessment

Assessment of the work that students do, and the way in which they do it, is basic to the educational process (Bredekamp and Rosegrant 1995; Perrone 1991). To genuinely teach children, we believe that we have to get to know children very well. Being aware of what a child knows, what he or she is capable of doing, and what he or she is like as a person gives us vital information. During the course of the school year, this information is useful as we decide what to teach and how to teach it.

The National Association for the Education of Young Children (NAEYC) offers eighteen principles (Bredekamp and Rosegrant 1995) that early childhood educators use to guide the way they assess young children. These guidelines promote the use of "an array of tools and a variety of processes" (23) in assessing "what children can do independently and what they can demonstrate with assistance since the latter shows the direction of their growth" (24). We agree with NAEYC that assessment of the whole child is basic to the educational process. "Children's development and learning in all domains—physical, social, emotional, and cognitive—and their dispositions and feelings are informally and routinely assessed by teachers' observing children's activities and interactions, listening to them as they talk, and using their constructive errors to understand their learning" (23). We use these NAEYC guidelines when we consider assessment of children as they plan and implement projects. Perhaps the most powerful methods of assessing young children begin with the tools teachers use to assess skills.

Assessing Skills

Teaching skills is an important part of Applied Learning projects. We embed skills in every project. We use different methods to track skills as they are taught, evaluate how well children learn them, and note the application of skills. These methods include checklists, rating scales, anecdotal records, and photographs.

Checklists

Checklists are an inventory of behaviors or skills. Lists like this focus our observations on a few associated behaviors. Marks on the checklist simply indicate whether a child exhibits a specific behavior during an observational period. We can mark checklists very quickly, so sometimes they are quite useful.

During project time, we would most likely use checklists to record skills being used to accomplish work related to the project. For example, if children were writing letters, we might use a checklist to record writing skills the children were exhibiting as they wrote. By the end of the year in a kindergarten class, these skills might include those in the following list, and would be marked as shown for the letter in Figure 8–1.

Letter Writing Skills Checklist

Check if skill is evident, leave blank if skill is not evident.

- ✔ hears and writes initial sound
- ✔ hears and writes initial and ending sound
- ✔ hears and writes medial vowel sounds
- ✔ uses periods to end sentences
- ✔ begins sentences with a capital letter
- ✔ uses spaces between words
- ✔ uses letter format
- ✔ communicates a clear message.

This list of writing skills could be used in any early childhood class. Not all assessments of project work have to be different from typical early childhood assessment. But, Applied Learning projects call for the assessment of both academic and nonacademic skills. We might work with the children to create a checklist of

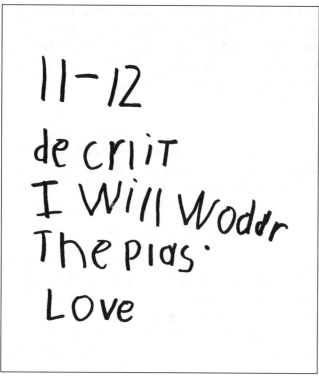

11-12
de crιιT
I Will Woddr
The pιαs.
Love

Figure 8–1. Child's Letter Promising to Water the Plants

behaviors expected for committee work as they create an end product. One list was created by a first-grade committee who was working on an exhibit brochure. Katy used this checklist to mark her observations, then had individual conferences with each child about committee behaviors. That checklist is shown in the following list:

Committee Work Checklist

___ listens to everyone's ideas in committee meetings
___ uses respectful language in committee meetings
___ has a reason to back up each opinion
___ accepts the group vote without complaining
___ does what is agreed to do at school
___ does what is agreed to do at home

From a Second-Grade Teacher . . .

I know that checklists aren't the end-all of assessment. They just don't get at the richness of project work. Still, I use them when I am trying to focus on the development of certain reading, writing, and mathematical skills. I see them as a quick glance at the levels where the children are working. Sometimes there are so many different things going on during project time that I have to focus my observations on one aspect of their work. Checklists help me do that.

The information provided by a checklist helps us identify certain skills that need to be encouraged for an individual or a group of children. For example, after completing the preceding checklists, we could identify the few children who still need support in leaving spaces between words or the child who still complains when a vote doesn't turn out his or her way. This bit of assessment directly influences instructional decisions.

Checklists can also be used to document a child's growth over time. When the same checklist is completed two or three different times over the course of the school year, progress is obvious. Viewed comparatively, these checklists offer a graphic depiction of a child's growth over time.

Checklists provide valuable information, but they also have limitations to consider. Because the behavior is either checked present or not present, there is no information about how well the child accomplished a task. Also, because young children do not consistently apply skills they are learning, you may not observe the use of a particular skill at a particular time, but the child may have been successful with it before.

Rating Scales

Rating scales are similar to checklists in that they focus the attention of the observer on specific behaviors and they are marked quickly (Tombari and Borich 1999). But rating scales go a step further than checklists by offering a way to document levels of performance. Because each marking requires a judgment on the part of the observer, we try not to let bias creep into our markings. Three-, five-, or seven-point scales are most often used to indicate the quality of the behavior being assessed. For example, in the research component of an Applied Learning project, we might decide to document students' dispositions toward research. The indicators might be:

- Exhibits curiosity and interest about the topic
- Asks questions about the topic
- Draws on past experience to make connections with current topic

We would mark each behavior on a three-point scale of "frequently," "sometimes," or "never"—or five-point or seven-point scale—being very deliberate about marking the indicators fairly (Puckett and Black 2000). Figures 8–2a and 8–2b show some sample rating scales.

119

Child: _____   Observer: _____

Age: _____   Date: _____

RATING SCALE
SOCIAL DEVELOPMENT

	Always	Sometimes	Never
In positive mood	3	2	1
Comes into classroom willingly	3	2	1
Is comforted rather quickly when upset	3	2	1
Expresses wishes, gives reasons	3	2	1
Expresses anger and frustrations in words	3	2	1
Gains access to ongoing groups at play and work	3	2	1
Accepted by most peers	3	2	1
Invited by other children to join them	3	2	1

Figure 8–2a. Sample Rating Scale

Child: _____   Observer: _____

Age: _____   Date: _____

RATING SCALE
LITERACY

	Always		Sometimes		Never
Likes to hear books read aloud	5	4	3	2	1
Independently chooses to look at books	5	4	3	2	1
Joins in on choral reading	5	4	3	2	1
Willing to "read"	5	4	3	2	1
Knows front cover and back cover	5	4	3	2	1
Holds books correctly	5	4	3	2	1
Turns pages one at a time, front to back	5	4	3	2	1
Knows what an author is	5	4	3	2	1
Knows what an illustrator is	5	4	3	2	1
Talks about personal drawings	5	4	3	2	1
Willing to "write"	5	4	3	2	1

Figure 8–2b.   Sample Rating Scale

© 2002 by Deborah Diffily and Charlotte Sassman from *Project-Based Learning with Young Children*. Portsmouth, NH: Heinemann.

Anecdotal Records to Document Skills

We also use anecdotal records to document our observations of children's developing skills. These records are brief, narrative descriptions of specific events (Grace and Shores 1991). We use informal anecdotal records to document the observation of a child—as he or she works alone, as she works collaboratively in small groups, or as he or she responds to shared experiences of the whole class. Usually informal anecdotal records are not appropriate for audiences beyond the teacher and the child's family. We use abbreviations frequently, so the notes may be unreadable to other people. Another reason we keep these notes private is because we write them quickly. The less-than-objective language may not provide the type of information that others should read.

Informal Anecdotal Records Typed Directly from Deborah's Notebook

1.9 DJ ≈ helps MS s-o words

1.12 DJ RD f-c "v" group

1.13 DJ sorts FLS ≈ accurate #/worm tubes—34

1.14 DJ ≈ BS, ME, and PL in ABC book re: R&F

Same Informal Anecdotal Records Transcribed

1.9 DJ offers to help sound out words for MS

1.12 DJ reads his fact cards to group working on "volcano rocks"

1.13 DJ sorts fossils and does an accurate count of the worm tubes—34

1.14 DJ leads group of BS, ME, and PL in beginning a group alphabet book about rocks and fossils

The abbreviated anecdotal records about DeVon (DJ) took only a moment to write. The notes reminded Deborah to continue observing how DeVon chose to collaborate with other children and when he chose to work alone. The week of January 12 was an important week for DeVon. These behaviors represented a major step in his social development. The notes were valuable when Deborah had a conference with DeVon's parents in mid-February. While few people could translate her compressed notes, they reminded Deborah of DeVon's newfound willingness to cooperate with classmates even though it occurred more than a month before the conference. Informal anecdotal records help us focus observations and also serve as a memory trigger for classroom events that deserve being shared with others.

Photographs

Photographs can document children's emerging skills as well as other aspects of project work. Keeping a camera loaded with film allows us to capture moments when children use skills as they work.

> **From a First-Grade Teacher . . .**
> I keep a Polaroid camera and a 35 mm camera in the room. I use both cameras as the situation dictates. When the children are working on an activity, I take a photo of what they are doing. Then they tell me what they were learning during that activity. I record this on paper and glue the photo to the top.

Photographs can also be used to document a child's progress over time. Some areas of project work are not easily documented. For example, part of project work can include building models of field trip sites or layouts of buildings. Paintings and drawings can be filed away quite easily. But, if a child decides to recreate a museum's layout through building a block structure, this cannot be put into a file. Photographs can document this part of project work, and as with other forms of documentation, comparative photographs demonstrate a child's growth very graphically. The evolution of a child's four-block structure created in August compared to the complex structures that are built in May cannot be easily described in words; however, a series of photographs clearly shows the child's growth. The same is true of other creative endeavors: sculptures, large murals, and "inventions." Photographs that are saved to demonstrate growth can be kept in folders along with other forms of assessment.

Documenting skills embedded during project work is important. However, equally important is the documentation of knowledge being acquired by students.

Assessing Knowledge

In Applied Learning classrooms, students develop significant knowledge. Much of the knowledge gained through projects is content related. It also includes processes such as learning ways to locate information, speaking before groups, etc. Assessment of knowledge gained by children during projects is best documented by authentic methods of evaluation (Helm, Beneke, and Steinheimer 1997). These methods often include a comparison of before-the-project dictation and end-of-the-project dictation, audiotapes, and videotapes.

Comparative Dictation

Cognitive psychologists believe that learners, even at the earliest grade levels, have some knowledge about nearly every topic they study. This information may be in the form of ideas (however vague), unconnected facts, implicit rules, or images. And often it may be wrong—what cognitive psychologists call misconceptions (Tombari and Borich 1999, 9).

We need to find out what facts are known and what misperceptions have been formed by children before a study begins. One way of gathering this information is to use basic interviewing techniques and record the child's comments. We either type a child's comments as he or she talks or audiotape the interview, transcribing the tape at a later time. A single question gives us an idea about each child's knowledge base. When that same question is asked after the project is complete, the comparison of the two dictations is quite telling. While this is not a totally accurate measure of everything known about a topic, comparing the two dictations gives a good idea of the content learned. An example is given in the comparative dictation that follows. Sometimes it is difficult for families to understand how much learning occurs during a project. These comparative interviews can show families—or even the children themselves—what has been learned during an Applied Learning project. "By the end of the year, the children . . . have a good self-concept about themselves" (Sassman, in Flagg 1998, 34).

Transcribing dictation from every child in the class can be time-consuming. Still, we think that comparing what children know before a project to what they know after the project is so powerful that the time is well spent.

Comparative Dictation from Travis about Plants

On January 26, Travis dictated the following:

Plants need rain. They grow by seeds. What they need to grow is sunshine, water, and soil.

On February 28, four weeks later, Travis dictated the following:

Trees grow bigger than whales like the California redwood and they live in California. Some trees have small seeds that can grow to be really bigger than you think could be growing from that little seed.

You need water, sunlight, and dirt and a seed to grow some plants and the way you can tell if it needs water is if the soil is dry. If it doesn't need water, the soil is a little wet.

Travis went on to describe different ways to start a seedling—from seeds, roots, bulbs, and sometimes just leaves. He described his favorite plants, the Venus fly trap and cactus. He discussed how people use parts of trees in different ways, then concluded with the following:

Sometimes when mushrooms come up to sprout out of the ground, they kind of look like eggs. Sometimes mushrooms are on pizzas and mushrooms mostly grow everywhere. We eat beans, apples, pears, celery, lettuce, coconuts. Most of these are plants. Some of them are fruits. Bananas are mainly a fruit but they grow on trees. Sometimes when people make clothes, they make it from some plants.

This comparison reveals several things about Travis's acquisition of knowledge. The focus of the project was deciding what plants would grow in a garden that the class would plant and care for. His interests went beyond the scope of the project, as he followed aspects about plants that he considered interesting.

Through his research, he developed a few misconceptions about plants that his teacher can address. He tends to recall information in a stream-of-consciousness manner, but he groups facts according to topic. He remembers correct names of those plants that captured his attention. He likes comparing objects. Perhaps the most important thing demonstrated by the comparison is that Travis obviously gained a wide range of knowledge about many different aspects of plants.

From a Kindergarten Teacher . . .
During my first project, I was a bit overwhelmed. These kids were learning things at such a rate that I just could not keep up with my documentation. I had been using the anecdotal records that I used the year before and I found myself trying to write down everything I noticed the children learning. I had to rethink how I was documenting what I observed. I did some reading about assessing project-based learning. I turned to using tapes for documentation and that freed up my time a lot. For my second project, I transcribed what children knew before we started the research, then I only wrote anecdotal records for the big things that stood out to me. When I took dictation from the students at the end of the project, even I was surprised at how much they had remembered.

Audiotapes

Audiotapes can record the before-the-project and end-of-the-project dictations, as well as other types of learning. We use audiotapes to record interviews with children, conversations between children during project work, and end-of-the-project presentations (only if the better option of videotaping is not available). We—and the children's family—can listen to the audiotapes and learn more about the development of a particular child. To make audiotaped information more accessible, we also transcribe the tapes. The transcript is then available for our analysis and/or for sharing with families.

Again, transcribing audiotapes takes time. We have spent many evenings at the computer, listening to tapes and typing what children recorded. We have also found that many people are willing to help us with this task. Parents who are particularly impressed with the before- and after-project dictations may help transcribe recordings. Preservice teachers studying assessment of young children often volunteer to transcribe audiotapes in exchange for conversations about what this kind of assessment shows about children's growth. In a pinch, we enlist friends or hire college students to transcribe audiotapes. This is not an assessment method we use frequently. We think one transcription per child every six to nine weeks is sufficient.

Videotapes

Videotapes also document children's behaviors in a variety of ongoing Applied Learning activities or in end-of-project presentations. With young children, it is advisable that an additional adult operate the camera so that the teacher can focus on the children's needs. If no volunteer can be found, a video camera set on a tripod can be left to run continuously, focused on a particular area of the classroom. However, sometimes the classroom noise overwhelms the specific conversation being recorded.

Using videos to compare beginning-of-school and end-of-school behaviors helps parents understand their child's progress or helps them envision what children do during the school day. A video of project work taken early in the year, compared to one taken toward the end of the year, can indicate longer attention spans, increased complexity of student work, and more cooperation and problem solving initiated by the students themselves. Comparative videos of a young child can demonstrate more sophisticated oral language, more attention to audience, and a greater command of the chosen topic. Videos can document growth in ways other methods of documentation cannot.

> **From a First-Grade Teacher . . .**
> In October, I lead my students through Independent Inquiries. The steps are similar to a project except that children work on their own. Each child chooses a topic, researches it, and creates an end product that shows what he or she learned. Each child makes a presentation to the rest of the class. Using one video per child, I tape the presentations. In May, children do a second Independent Inquiry, and I videotape that presentation [on the same cassette] immediately following the first one. During the end-of-the-year conferences, the parents, the child, and I watch the video. Parents are always amazed at the progress their child has made. The children are even impressed with themselves. Videotaping these presentations takes little time, and families are pleased to have this kind of reminder of first grade.

Beyond simple documentation of knowledge, these methods of assessment provide a window to the learning in Applied Learning projects. Families see this information as helpful in understanding their child's learning because the learning is graphically portrayed for them to see. When children compare the transcribed lists of what was dictated about a topic before and after a project, they understand that they learned "a whole lot." Audio- and videotapes "enable children to revisit experiences and provide a basis for discussing the project experiences and reflecting on what was learned" (Helm, Beneke, and Steinheimer 1997, 67). Assessment of skills and knowledge gained during Applied Learning projects is rounded out by the assessment of the children's dispositions and feelings.

Assessing Dispositions and Feelings

Children's disposition to use newly acquired skills and knowledge and their feelings about their work are just as important as the expanded skills and knowledge. We use anecdotal records and interviews as perhaps the best methods of documenting children's dispositions.

Anecdotal Records to Document Dispositions and Feelings

Again, we simply cannot rely on our memories to recall the numerous events that occur in an early childhood class. This is especially true regarding children's dispositions and feelings. Without some form of documentation, we might remember days that a child seemed hesitant about working with committee members, documenting learning, or helping make group decisions, but we could not pinpoint the particular days we observed these behaviors. All children have days when they are not feeling particularly positive about their work, but when negative feelings become a pattern, it is time to investigate possible reasons. We document moments that indicate a change in feelings or dispositions rather than all the feelings or dispositions of each child. We share these observations with families, both positive and negative. Special comments children make as they are responding to read-alouds, the varied ways they use materials for research, and the comments they say to each other are frequently occurrences worthy of documentation. Here is a sample anecdotal record:

Informal Anecdotal Records Typed Directly from Charlotte's Notebook
1.8   HR ≈ KC, AN, TM on cls brochure, WTS! 1 for this
1.9   " " " "
1.12   " " ?? HR wont WT, very quiet in G ??
         no lunch ??
1.13   PT ≈ alone, draws, trashes P, repeat
1.14   WW & PT ≈ no W, tears, suns

Same Informal Anecdotal Records Transcribed
1.8   Heather works with Katherine, Annetta, and Tyler on class brochure. The group has worked together many times, but this time, Heather takes on the role of writer. This is the first time Heather has volunteered to write for the group.
1.9   The same group of girls works together for the second day and, again, Heather writes the copy for the group's drawings for the brochure.
1.12   After morning meeting, Heather joins the same group of girls. When they assume that she will write for the group as she had the week before, Heather says she doesn't want to. She says almost nothing as the group continues to work on the class brochure. Heather is also very quiet at lunch and eats almost nothing.

1.13   During project time, Heather chooses not to join the group she has been working with. She takes a clipboard to a corner of the room and begins to draw. After a few minutes, she tears the picture in half and puts it in the recycling bin. She returns to the corner, draws for a few minutes, and then puts that piece of paper in the recycling bin. She talks to no one and seems quite sad.

1.14   Today Heather does not write at all during writing workshop and project time. She sits at a table with paper and markers in front of her, but does not write words or draw pictures. Occasionally, she draws sun-like objects, but never expands beyond those figures.

These anecdotal records document a positive change in Heather's disposition to write and then reflect a rather dramatic reversal in both disposition and feelings. On Monday, Charlotte noted the apparent change in Heather's behavior and attitudes. Going on the assumption that everybody has a bad day sometimes, she just observed and documented her observations. On Tuesday afternoon, Charlotte found a quiet moment toward the end of project time and asked if Heather had a minute to talk. She said, "Heather, it seems to me that you are sad today. Can we talk about it?" Heather said, "Yes," she was sad. While her eyes filled with tears, she said nothing was wrong, that she was just sad. Charlotte hugged her, acknowledged that everyone has sad days from time to time and reassured Heather that she is always available to talk. When the pattern of behavior continued, Charlotte called Heather's mom and talked about her observations. Sue, Heather's mom, said that she had not noticed any change in Heather's behavior at home but that she would talk with Heather that night. Sue had a long talk with Heather. After a long chat, Heather finally told her mother that over the weekend, one of her cousins—a teenager whom Heather looked up to—had referred to her writing as scribble-scrabble. As a young kindergartner, Heather's handwriting was not particularly neat and her spelling was rudimentary, but this comment hurt Heather deeply and she responded by withdrawing from the act of writing.

The documentation of Heather's dispositions and feelings helped Charlotte recognize the developing pattern. Bringing her observations to the parent helped get at the root of Heather's out-of-the-ordinary behavior. Knowing how hurt Heather had been by her cousin's comment helped Charlotte support Heather and rebuild her confidence. Teachers and parents can often find out about children's dispositions and feelings simply by talking to them.

Interviews

Interviews with children provide great insight into how they perceive their world. An interview might be as simple as sitting down in the writing center and saying to the children working there, "Can you tell me about what you are writing?" Or we may ask children in the reading center what they think about the book they are reading. Quick notes reflecting the children's responses provide information about how children think and how they view their work.

In more formal interviews, we decide in advance what questions to ask the children. This formal interview format gives us more information about children and provides insight into a child's thoughts and feelings. As mentioned earlier in this chapter, repeating an assessment allows us, the child, and the child's family to compare the child's responses from one time period to another, adding to the depth of understanding the child.

From a Kindergarten Teacher . . .
I use formal interviews to assess children's literacy knowledge during the first few days of school. I photocopy my question sheet, leaving space to write the child's answer after each one. I ask the children about books, magazines, and newspapers in the home and who reads them. I ask about a favorite book and ask the child to retell the story.

When I asked Mark if he had books at his home, he answered, "Yes." To the question "Does your mom read books?" he answered, "She reads her school books." When I asked "Does your dad read books?" he waited a long time, clearly thinking. Then he seriously responded, "Well, he has a checkbook." The things you learn from listening to children's responses!

When working on projects, it is important to understand how children feel about their work and their interactions with their groups. Often a child's misconception will go unnoticed unless we listen very carefully to the child. Simple questions encourage children to talk about their feelings about project work, such as:

- "How did you feel when your family came to see our museum/video/class book?"
- "What part of the project do you feel most proud of?"
- "What part of this project was the hardest/easiest for you?"
- "Who helped you do serious work? Why did you pick that person?"

We occasionally take notes as children reply to such questions; however, documenting the child's entire response with a hand-held tape recorder is preferable. We transcribe the remarks and make the transcription available at conferences. This transcription is time-consuming, but it is much easier for the parents, and us, to evaluate when the interviews are transcribed.

Not only is this evaluation of knowledge, skills, dispositions, and feelings important, but also the evaluation of a project's product(s) is important.

Evaluation of Work Products

Throughout an Applied Learning project, there are many opportunities for us—and the children themselves—to evaluate the work that is done. We establish criteria; then the work is assessed. Methods of assessing work created during projects include lists of criteria, rubrics, and the children's self-assessment; and carefully constructed portfolios.

Criteria

The term *criteria* is used to describe a list of characteristics that make a particular kind of work acceptable or good. A list of criteria is usually developed jointly by the teacher and students and relates to a specific type of work within an Applied Learning project. Most often criteria are agreed on before the children begin work. They examine a model to establish what they will be working toward. After looking at proposals submitted to the principal by other classes, second graders decided that their proposal should have at least five things so it would be a good proposal. The criteria to guide their drafts of the proposal are shown here.

Proposal Criteria
- States request in the first paragraph
- Has several reasons to back up request
- Uses conventional spelling
- Has all words spelled correctly
- Says thank you at end of letter

Criteria are established as the children work on specific parts of a project. The criteria focus children's attention on improving their work. In the first-grade Reptile Museum Exhibit, the children were drawing pictures of reptiles, having already decided that these pictures would be included in their exhibit. Several children seemed to be more interested in drawing lots of pictures instead of concentrating on the quality of the pictures. Deborah led the class through a discussion about what a "great picture" would look like. The class developed the criteria listed in the Great Pictures list that follows. The children returned to previous drawings and revised them to meet the criteria. Three of these drawings are shown in Figure 8–3a, b, and c.

Great Pictures
- Real reptiles, no pretend ones
- Lots of color
- Page filled with color, no white spaces
- Lots of detail in drawing

Figure 8–3a. "Great" Pictures

Figure 8–3b. "Great" Pictures

Figure 8–3c. "Great" Pictures

Sometimes criteria are also used to help children identify social behaviors that make one a good committee member, a self-controlled person, a serious worker, a good reader, a good writer, and so on. The following Good Committee Members list shows the criteria developed by a class of first graders.

Good Committee Members
- Wait for a turn to talk
- Listen to the other people

- Think about what the other person says before responding
- Compromise
- Be responsible for completing the jobs
- Stay on the topic; don't goof around
- Look at the speaker
- Keep up with all the work
- Share the work with everyone
- Take turns

Criteria can be developed for virtually any work product produced or social behavior exhibited during project time. However, there are times when a list of characteristics is not enough. Rubrics are then used to differentiate among levels of work.

Rubrics

In addition to listing criteria, a rubric provides a scoring scale and a written description of each level of each criterion (Lewin and Shoemaker 1998). "The development of rubrics helps to focus observations and assessments on the essentials and assists both learners and teachers in defining progress and quality" (Puckett and Black 2000, 233).

Rubrics help students understand what is expected before they begin work and guide the assessment of their work. Well-written rubrics "can improve student performance as well as monitor it" (Goodrich 1996/97, 2). We post the rubrics in the classroom, referring students to them to evaluate their own and each other's work more realistically. Rubrics tie the child's evaluations to clear descriptions of quality.

Rubrics also guide us in providing specific feedback to children as they work. We review the descriptors point by point, helping students understand what is needed to improve the work product. Examples of high-quality student work that meets all the high-point descriptions guide students as they improve their work. We specifically teach students the skills of self-evaluation and reflection about their work, using the rubrics as a standard.

Good rubrics are not particularly easy to write. The language of the descriptions needs to be very clear so that everyone in the class interprets the language the same way (Sassman, in Flagg 1998). With young children, this usually means putting the descriptors in the words of the children themselves.

In kindergarten and first-grade classes, our rubrics have only two levels for each criterion. At first, the work is judged in a yes/no manner, but as the children have more experiences, rubrics are extended to three- or four-point scales, such as:

- Never, sometimes, consistently
- Not yet, in process, proficient
- Beginner, developing, competent
- Working on, demonstrated some of the time, effectively demonstrated
- Minimum, good, excellent, exceptional
- Needs improvement, basic, good, commendable
- Emergent, beginning, developing, proficient

Criteria for Details in Reports

4 - Enough details to give the reader a clear understanding of the subject

3 - Some details are included, but some important details are missing

2 - Not enough details are included, but there are a few

1 - Almost no details

While children develop their rubrics with us, they learn to assess their own work or performances. Reflecting about their work and making self-assessments are the next step.

Children's Reflection/Self-Assessment

Children's self-assessments are statements made to explain what they think about their work. Experts (Bredekamp and Rosegrant 1995; Farr and Tone 1994) encourage early childhood educators to involve their students in self-assessment activities. While young children's early self-assessments are not necessarily accurate—according to adult perspectives—making decisions about their work's quality adds to the sense of ownership they have for their work. We find young children need many experiences in self-assessment in order to honestly assess their capabilities and work products.

Children tend to make statements "based on their perceptions about what makes work good" (Puckett and Diffily 1999, 146). Young children's early self-assessments tend to be broad statements such as, "I did good," or "I worked hard." They think their work is good because "it's got all the colors," or because "I worked hard on it and because the name is neat." We guide children to move beyond this initial stage of self-assessment. Bickart, Jablon, and Dodge (1999) suggest asking children specific questions to help them think more critically about their work. They recommend questions such as:

- "What do you like best about your drawing?"
- "How do you decide if you like a story you write, or a picture you draw?"
- "What did you enjoy most about this project?"
- "Which math problem was frustrating? Why?"
- "What was most difficult for you to do? What was easy to do?"

- "Did you try using a new technique in writing your story?"
- "What's the hardest part of working in a group?" (202)

We ask additional questions that relate specifically to committee work and planning:

- "How well did your group work today?"
- "How did you contribute to the committee's work?"
- "How did you accomplish _____ (a specific task)?"
- "Did you stick with the plan you made this morning?"
- "How well did your group accomplish this week's goals?"

Children need multiple experiences in assessing their own work. They develop more sophisticated assessment of their own work when we guide them with questions and as they learn to use criteria and rubrics to judge work products. After nine months of learning to assess her own work, Julia dictated her thoughts about herself as a reader and writer:

> I think that I have learned very much in kindergarten. I can read a whole lot of books and I can write just about anything I want to write. I never thought I could read so many books, but I can and I am still getting better at reading hard books like Tomie dePaola and maybe even Bill Martin Jr. I am going to read chapter books next year. I really think I can and I will write even harder books, like chapter books, next year too because now I can write long books and I draw real good and my friends like my illustrations and they like my stories. On the first day of school, I could only write names, and now I can write books and that is the very best that I could do."

When we introduce the idea of self-assessment to children, we usually introduce yes/no evaluations, such as "Did I listen during storytime?" or "Did I try to sound out words for my story today?" As children develop the ability to judge dichotomous behaviors, we expand self-assessment. Five- and six-year-olds can describe how they are good listeners when others are talking. They can evaluate their participation in a group activity, how cooperative they are, and what they might change in future group work. They can analyze their own work and then discuss what makes it good and what they think they need to work on next.

Children, six-, seven- or eight-years-old who have become rather fluent writers respond to their work by writing simple self-assessments. We provide half sheets of paper with these phrases already written on them:

This piece shows that I can _____.
Next time I will _____.

Figure 8–4 shows one of these self-assessments. Students can work alone or in pairs to complete these self-assessments. Paired students help each other recognize the

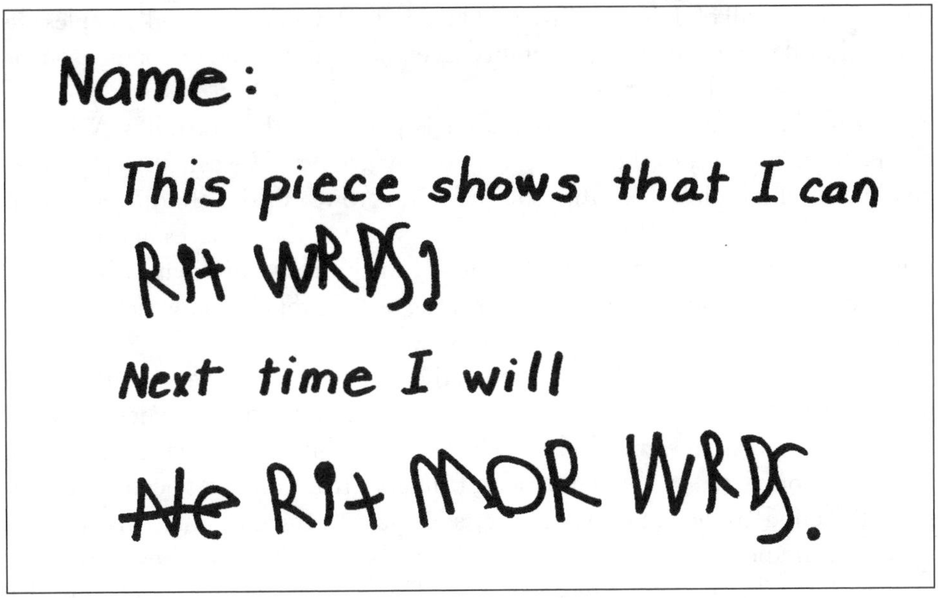

Name:

This piece shows that I can

RIt WRDS)

Next time I will

~~Ae~~ RIt MOR WRDS.

Figure 8–4. Self-Assessment of Writing

things they do well and remember the class goals for that particular piece of work. This simple form leads children to state the knowledge or skills that are evident in a work sample and helps them plan ahead by looking for specific ways to improve their work.

Self-assessment of completed work and self-reflections about the process of working on a project are learning experiences in and of themselves. However, when they are collected and reviewed on a regular basis, they show a child's growth very clearly. Comparing self-reflections made early in the school year to self-reflections made later in the year helps children realize their progress and feel successful. The same is true for early work compared to later work. We organize and store comparative work samples, documentation of our observations, and children's self-assessments in a single, centralized location, such as in a portfolio.

Portfolios

Student portfolios are particularly effective in documenting project work completed by each student. A portfolio is "a purposeful collection of student work that exhibits the student's efforts, progress, and achievements in one of more areas" (Paulson, Paulson, and Meyer 1991, 60). Portfolios also include documentation of a teacher's observations: anecdotal records, checklists, rating scales, interviews, notes about children's work, photographs, audiotapes, and videotapes, but do not have to include all of these (Diffily and Fleege 1993). Children's work samples are also included to indicate a child's ability level, or when viewed in comparison, as indicators of a child's progress.

We make some decisions about what is placed in the portfolios. We may choose to include any of the items previously mentioned. We can also select specific pieces of a child's work that showcase the growth of the child over several months. We explain to the child why we've selected those pieces and what we think they show about him or her. We model the process—reviewing several options, making a portfolio selection, and stating reasons for choosing the piece—to teach the children to make these decisions alone.

Students also select work to include in the portfolio. Often we encourage children to select their best work to put in portfolios. At other times, students choose favorite work, most meaningful work, or the most difficult or challenging work they have completed in a given period of time. After making a selection for the portfolio, children dictate or write entry slips, stating the reason(s) why they selected certain pieces for their portfolios. They also identify what they think they learned doing that particular piece of work. These entry slips are attached to the work, then it is placed into portfolios.

Younger children, or students without much experience in this process, tend to give rather simplistic reasons for selecting a piece of work. They often choose work based on personal preferences: "I picked this story cause it is about a dog and I like dogs," or "I like this book because it has stamps and stamps are really neat to me actually. I picked it because it had stamps in it and I liked it."

As children practice doing this, they become more sophisticated in the process. They begin making more realistic selections and offer more reasoned rationales. The rationales just mentioned were all dictated by one kindergarten student. As a first grader, he gave such rationales as: "This is my script for the videotape for Stephanie's class. I picked it because I like it and I worked hard on it and I put periods and spaces between words. And I writed neatly so other people could read it and did not mess up. I learned how to do scripts and I learned how to do a videotape and I learned to make lots of words." Making portfolio selections that demonstrate the growth and learning and offering reasoned rationales develop over time. Selecting work to be placed in a portfolio and giving reasons for choosing a particular piece of work helps children learn to value their own work and is an important tool in developing self-directed learners.

Grades

The majority of project teachers use the methods of assessment just discussed. Some of these teachers write narrative reports to summarize the progress of their students. Others must translate these more authentic methods of assessment into letter or number grades to place on required report cards. At first, this seems difficult. However, if rubrics and lists of criteria are routinely used to evaluate work products, grades can be derived. A four-point rubric could be used to arrive at A, B, C, and D grades. More than one rubric can be developed for one work sample. For example, to evaluate children's research for a science-related Applied Learning project, one rubric could be developed to assess knowledge gained and another to assess conventions of writing. Thus, a science grade and an English grade could be recorded from one work sample.

Lists of criteria can also be used to "grade" student work. Returning to the criteria developed by second-grade students to evaluate proposals, there were five established criteria. Each criterion could be assigned twenty points and scored accordingly for a total possible score of one hundred points. The same is true for the criteria for good committee members created by the first-grade class. If the ten criteria were assigned ten points each, then an evaluation could be made and scored for a possible one hundred points. While grades may not be the preferred method of reporting assessment results, the need for grades does not coerce us to give up the more authentic methods of assessment.

Summary

Assessment plays a fundamental role in project-based classrooms. Teacher observation of young children is a powerful assessment method. These observations are documented with checklists, rating scales, anecdotal records, and/or photographs. Applied Learning teachers assess children's acquisition of knowledge and the enhancement of their skills. They also evaluate how children feel about their work and whether they are inclined to use the skills they are learning. Teachers and students both use pre-established criteria and rubrics to judge behaviors and specific work products. The information we learn through observation and evaluation of their work is used to plan instruction, share children's progress with families, and evaluate the curriculum's effectiveness.

9

Parting Words of Advice

Good to go.

—*Apollo 13*, the movie

From the time we first saw the movie *Apollo 13*, we've wanted to be in a situation where we could use the phrase, "Good to go." This seems as appropriate as any time. You've read about our experiences with Applied Learning projects. Now it is your turn to experiment with this approach to teaching and learning with young children. This chapter contains just a few more words of advice.

Deciding to start a first project with young children is a risk-taking endeavor. Even if you have had a child-centered classroom for years, there is something different about Applied Learning projects and classrooms. Allowing young children to make decisions about what to learn and how to present their learning to people outside the classroom is child directed, a step beyond child centered. In previous chapters, we shared what we think are the benefits of project-based learning and detailed the general course of projects.

Yet, this is not the "book of answers" for implementing projects with young children. There are simply too many variables in a project that cannot be controlled. The way a project progresses is influenced by the teacher, the children in the class, the project's topic, the number of resources that can be located, and the end product that the class chooses. Throughout your first project—and to some extent, during every project you undertake—you will be "feeling your way," making the best decision you can at the time, considering all the factors involved in your community of learners.

Our best advice to you at this point is trust the children, trust yourself, and for those moments of confusion or frustration, find a like-minded colleague to talk with.

Trust the Children

It is hard to break the old, seemingly universal, arrangement where adults know what is best and children follow the directions of adults. In many cases, that old adage is still true. It is true in cases involving safety or when there is no time for a group meeting and a quick decision must be made. However, most of the time, children make good decisions when the question is framed appropriately, and sometimes children come up with ideas that we would never think of. Given a rich environment and the empowerment to make decisions, children make some very interesting decisions.

From a Kindergarten Teacher . . .
I used to pride myself in being able to solve all the children's problems. I thought I was helping children see that there is a solution to every problem, but I was always the one with the solution. "Let Jonathan play in the sand center first, then it can be your turn." "Let's divide the markers so you'll each have your own colors and you won't have to argue." "You sit by the window and he can sit by the door. Then you both can do your work." I've learned through project work that children can solve most of their problems on their own, if I just hold back a little. Now I ask more questions such as, "What are some ways you can resolve this argument?" "What could you do differently next time to keep this from happening again?" and "I'm not sure. What do you think?" My role as a problem solver is just as important as before, but now I guide the children and trust that they will come up with solutions to their own problems whether the problems are related to conflicts with other people or related to their learning. I really think I am teaching more now than I was before.

During the Reptile Exhibit project, several children got together and made a decision that surprised Deborah and the children's families. One morning, for shared reading time, Deborah read Jerry Pallotta's *The Yucky Reptile Alphabet Book* (1989). The children seemed to enjoy the book and they commented frequently during the read-aloud about facts they were still learning. However, during the afternoon class meeting, David announced that the people at his lunch table talked about the book. They decided that they absolutely did not want to put Pallotta's book in their exhibit. They wanted "to put books in the exhibit so people could know about books that would help people learn more about reptiles. And Pallotta's book has a lie in it." A few children backed up David, condemning Pallotta for calling reptiles "yucky." They insisted they "knew a lot about reptiles, and some of them are strange, but no reptile was yucky." David called for a class vote, and within minutes, the class voted unanimously to outlaw *The Yucky Reptile Alphabet Book* from their museum. Several children announced that they would create their own reptile alphabet books to exhibit. On their own, the children discussed what they saw as a problem, presented it at a class meeting, and came up with their own solution. It is not always easy to trust young children, and they are certainly not this impressive during every moment of project work. Still, trusting children is an important underlying principle for successful work in Applied Learning projects.

Trust Yourself

Not only should you trust the children, you need to trust yourself too. Reflect on your strengths as an early childhood educator. You understand the principles of child growth and development. You carefully observe children to discover what they know and what they can do. You build learning experiences that start "where the children are" and help move them forward. You believe that all children can learn and go about setting up an environment that supports that learning, and plan active experiences that help children "construct their own knowledge." In reality, you are quite knowledgeable about early childhood education and how young children learn best.

You are already familiar with much of what we've discussed in these chapters. Even if some of the roles of an Applied Learning teacher are new to you, you are obviously interested in being the best teacher you can be. Learning a few new ways of interacting with children is certainly something that you can do.

Both of us are early childhood educators by choice. We love working with five-, six-, and seven-year-olds. There is something magic about children's learning at this age. We love watching young children as they learn to read and write. We've always been fascinated with this process. Since we have worked with children in project work, we are even more fascinated with them as we watch them develop the skills to justify their opinions and negotiate differences. It is gratifying to listen to them explain a problem and even more gratifying to hear others in the class brainstorm possible solutions, then go through the process of choosing the best one. Perhaps the greatest sense of pride for us is standing back and observing our students sharing the end product they created. Watching young children who are so confident in their knowledge stand in front of much older audiences and talk about reptiles—or whatever topic they chose—and then field questions with ease is one of those moments that reassures us that teaching young children is the best of professions.

> **From a First-Grade Teacher . . .**
> My class volunteered to help third-grade students with one of their projects. The third graders planned and sponsored a Young Authors Conference for our school dis-

trict. During the planning stages, they realized they needed help. When we agreed to help, they asked us to be responsible for inviting all the local school officials. Imagine my concern when we got a message that the superintendent wanted to talk to someone about the invitation we had sent. I knew that the children needed to return this phone call, and I wanted them to. But it was to the superintendent! Of course it turned out well, Kyle was poised and fielded all the questions well while the superintendent was supportive and caring. Still, letting a six-year-old talk to the man that signs your paycheck can be a little intimidating!

Still, not every moment of project work fills us with lofty, fulfilling feelings. There are moments when we get frustrated or feel confused or think that maybe, just maybe, we should be doing some kind of other work. But then, that is life and, after all, life is what we are teaching the children.

Find a Colleague to Talk With

When those less-than-satisfying moments do occur, it helps to talk to someone who understands. Anyone trying out a new set of behaviors finds that a support system is helpful. This is particularly true when trying project-based learning for the first time. There are few clear answers to problems that come up during projects, so it helps to talk with a like-minded colleague who understands the nature of project work. Sometimes just talking out concerns helps you reach your own decision. Sometimes a sentence or two that someone else says will prompt a new way of thinking about a problem. But it is important to choose the right person to talk to. It's best if it's someone who works with young children and agrees with your philosophy about how children learn best.

From a Kindergarten Teacher . . .
I found myself talking to my husband about the project I was working on with my kindergarten students. I would describe something that had come up in class. I wanted him to talk with me about possible solutions, but it didn't take me long to figure out that he really didn't care to weigh options. He just wanted to tell me how to solve the problem. That didn't help. And, none of my close friends were teachers. Even though they tried, they just didn't "get" that what I was talking about were real problems. No one else in my building was doing projects. They all thought I was just a little weird. I was beginning to give up on projects. There was just too much I didn't understand about when to push kids and when to support them; when to offer resources, when to wait. Then things changed. At an inservice, I met a first-grade teacher who was struggling with the whole notion of what it means to let children

lead the projects. We began a friendship. Our telephone conversations over the next year helped me tremendously. Neither of us had all the answers, but just talking about the details of projects with someone who truly understood my questions kept me going. And, you know what? It was worth it.

It helps to have someone to talk with about the parts of a project that go well, but more important to have someone to talk through the parts that do not go as expected. Sometimes, a teacher not directly involved in your project can see options not obvious to you. There are times during the implementation of any project that you will need to talk through issues with someone.

From a Second-Grade Teacher . . .

Before I started doing projects with children, there weren't too many unexpected problems that came up in my classroom. I had taught second grade for ten years. I knew seven- and eight-year-olds. I could plan activities that they liked and learned from. I anticipated most problems and knew before they happened what I would do. But projects changed all that! There were days when it seemed as if nothing ran smoothly. Children argued over resources. They couldn't agree on how they wanted to present information to others. They would argue over little things like the color of the posterboard they were going to use in a display. At first, I saw this all as chaos. It was hard for me to accept that children solving these problems was a good idea. Eventually I came to understand that the children were learning important skills as they solved these problems. Solving small problems as young children prepares children for solving larger and more complex problems later.

Applied Learning projects are rich learning experiences and Applied Learning classrooms offer an incredible learning environment for children. Providing this is not always easy to do, but then we think there are lots of things in life that are not easy. Not easy, but the results are well worth the effort. As the ancient Chinese philosopher Lao-tzu said, "A journey of a thousand miles must begin with a single step." Applied Learning is how we help young children begin their journey.

Final Words from Deborah

I came to the concept of Applied Learning projects with a strong early childhood education background. As a prekindergarten, kindergarten, and first-grade teacher, I tried to follow the teaching principles established by the National Association for the Education of Young Children. So I was accustomed to offering children options, encouraging them to self-select materials I organized in learning centers, and supporting their development of self-control. I had already used project-based learning in my kindergarten classes. I believed that I was a good teacher for young children.

When I first learned about the concept of Applied Learning projects, I was not convinced that this was "best practice" for five- and six-year-olds. I questioned the need to connect projects to the real world and argued that projects should only be connected to the child's world. I contended that the audience for the end product did not have to be a real audience. I thought that, for young children, a perceived audience was sufficient. And, as much as I believed in a child-centered class, I was a bit skeptical about child-directed projects. After all, I was teaching five-year-olds.

For months, I held onto my previous definition of projects. I was experienced. After all, my kindergartners had walked to a grocery store and drawn pictures, then made their own grocery store at school, working over several days. I had observed the learning involved in that project and was impressed with what five-year-olds learned as they created a grocery store.

Because I had committed to trying Applied Learning projects, I felt I had to implement at least one. My first project was a failure, pure and simple. I started it before working out some logistical details, and when the children had to wait three weeks for the field trip I had "pondered" them into, they lost all interest. I could not regenerate any interest in the topic. I pushed too hard to get children to "choose" a project. After that failure, I relaxed. I forced myself to observe students and wait until they expressed an interest in a topic. Our second project was the Rock and Fossil Exhibit project discussed at length in Chapter 5. This project convinced me about the value of Applied Learning projects.

I was so impressed at the number of facts the children learned—and remembered. Their reading and writing efforts improved dramatically during the seven weeks we spent on this project. But most impressive to me was the way the children handled themselves when they acted as docents in our museum. Gone were the shy kindergartners. They answered questions asked by older students and adults alike, and when they couldn't remember an answer, they confidently stated, "I believe David (or the name of another child) knows more about than I do. Let's check with him."

Throughout the writing of this book, the faces and the voices of children have been in the back of my mind. I've thought about how:

- The boy who only knew hitting and biting as a way of getting what he wanted learned—over time—to use words to explain, negotiate, and compromise

- The boy who spent the first six weeks of Writers' Workshop crying under a table wrote his own book of poetry, a twenty-page autobiography, and a play before he left first grade
- The girl who was such a perfectionist in kindergarten that she initially led every small group by telling others what to do and by announcing the solution to every problem in large-group meetings but, toward the end of kindergarten, leaned over to me and whispered, "I won't be talking in class meeting today. I need to give other people a chance to express what they think."
- The shy girl who held onto her mother's skirt for the first few weeks of kindergarten developed into a confident first grader who stood in front of 2,000 people at a conference on adoption and talked about how it felt to be adopted

These are only four of the children I taught. They all made amazing progress from the day they walked into the kindergarten class until the time they left first grade. I credit that progress to the learning introduced and supported through the process of Applied Learning projects.

Final Words from Charlotte

I taught first grade for fifteen years in a school that is recognized as being a "good school." I was successful, managing my class efficiently and teaching the needed skills. My children passed the "test"—they could walk quietly down the hall and behaved in the lunchroom (or else I followed through with the consequences I had told them about). I posted attractive class work outside my door with each child's work looking very much like the others. My classroom was arranged in four straight rows with little pouches on the side of each desk to hold that child's supplies. I could walk down one aisle and up the other, quickly checking the work while stamping each child's page with a smiling happy face (or, horrors, a frowning sad face). When the children tattled to me, I immediately solved their problems. All the "learning" occurred when I told the children what to do and when to do it. I had not thought about involving the children in making decisions or directing their own learning. I just saw to it that the children finished each textbook before the end of the year.

Something bugged me about the way I was teaching. Now I approach teaching and learning in an entirely different way. I have worked as an Applied Learning teacher for ten years, and now I follow the children instead of leading them, include them in all the decisions made in the classroom instead of deciding for them, and let them "walk with a friend" to lunch instead of down the hall in a single, straight line. Few children tattle, because they know my response will be "what have you done to solve this problem?" My children still behave and they still learn the necessary skills. But I feel much better about what goes on in my classroom. Now the children construct their own knowledge, manipulating it until they understand it.

I realize teaching is more than following a prepared lesson plan or guideline from a textbook. It is observing the children to see what they need and providing that for them. It is knowing the behaviors of young children and creating learning experiences that support that behavior.

From someone who had fifteen years of traditional teaching, take my advice. Give project work a chance—it might change your life.

Appendix A

The History of Projects in American Education

As defined by the National Association for the Education of Young Children, appropriate programs for young children

> result from the process of professionals making decisions about the well-being and education of children based on at least three important kinds of information or knowledge: 1. what is known about child development and learning, 2. what is known about the strengths, interests, and needs of each individual child in the group, 3. knowledge of the social and cultural contexts in which children live (Bredekamp and Copple 1997, 8–9).

Projects fit within this framework of developmentally appropriate practices for young children and the teaching method of child-selected projects is certainly not a new concept. Projects were used in the Lab School at the University of Chicago as early as 1896 (Tanner 1997). Projects were described as early as 1918 when William Heard Kilpatrick published "The Project Method" in the *Teachers College Record*.

In 1926, projects were an important part of two different presentations to the National Society for the Study of Education. Flora Cooke, the principal of the Francis Parker School in Chicago, said:

> We believe that self-actuated work results in the greatest gain to the pupil and therefore we seek to encourage self-initiated individual and small group projects to foster special interests and to allow time for such activity on the regular school program (Cooke 1926, 306).

Caroline Pratt, founder of the City and Country School in New York City, also discussed the projects used at her school:

147

The essential difference between our method and any project method with which I am familiar lies in the fact that ours is not merely a school method. It is a method which can be applied to adult social undertakings and is often applied to informal undertakings. It is a method of learning to live and work together (Pratt 1926, 332).

A few years later, Lucy Sprague Mitchell (1934/1971) wrote about using projects in her school to teach geography, an area of study that she thought was being neglected in schools. She believed strongly in the value of the community for providing genuine opportunities for learning. In *Young Geographers: How They Explore the World and How They Map the World*, Mitchell described how children made decisions about what they would study, how they used a wide variety of sources, and how much her teachers valued children's exploration of a topic. She wrote, "It is only by exploring the 'here and now' that children grow in the capacity to discover relations—to think" (Mitchell 1934/1971, 23). She viewed projects as a primary way to encourage children's thinking.

Projects are not only supported by historical early childhood educators, they are well grounded in the work of educational theorists:

- Jean Piaget's proposition about children constructing their own knowledge (Piaget 1936/1952)
- Lev Vygotsky's conjecture about how language drives thought and thus conversations influence cognitive development (Vygotsky 1934/1986)
- John Dewey's belief that learning comes through real-world learning experiences in a child-centered curriculum (Dewey 1938)
- Howard Gardner's explanation of multiple intelligences and how these intelligences can be used in the classroom to better meet children's needs (Gardner 1983, 1993).

Appendix B

Books About Project-Based Learning

There are many different approaches to project-based learning. These books represent different uses of projects.

> Chard, Sylvia. 1998. *The Project Approach: Making Curriculum Come Alive (Book 1)*. New York: Scholastic.
> ———. 1998. *The Project Approach: Managing Successful Projects (Book 2)*. New York: Scholastic.

These two books offer insight into the Project Approach as defined by Katz and Chard in Engaging Children's Minds: The Project Approach *(2000). Book One discusses curriculum issues—reviewing classroom practices such as how teachers teach children, how children best learn, how the environment is arranged, and how content is integrated. It also describes the phases of the Project Approach, explains projects from the learner's point of view, and discusses the roles of the people involved. Book Two addresses management issues—getting started, developing and concluding projects, and organizing the classroom. Both books offer sample plans and examples for using projects with children in K–5. Additional mention is made of projects involving older children.*

> Edwards, Carolyn P., Lella Gandini, and George Forman, eds. 1998. *The Hundred Languages of Children: The Reggio Emilia Approach—Advanced Reflections*. 2d ed. Greenwich, CT: Ablex.

This book portrays the Reggio Emilia philosophy of intellectual development—addressing the needs of the whole child in all-encompassing child care and educational settings within a highly collaborative problem-solving approach to learning. Each chapter presents a different view—educators from Reggio Emilia explain their program, theory and practice are presented, and implications for American classrooms are addressed.

149

Gardner, Howard. 1998. *Project Spectrum: Project Zero Frameworks for Early Childhood Education*. Vol. 1. New York: Teachers College Press.

A collaboration between Tufts University and Harvard University brought about the notion of Project Spectrum, initially a search for more authentic ways to assess young children's strengths across developmental domains. This approach to projects is more related to hands-on activities that are highly engaging to children—themes that can be addressed in school and museum settings and revisited over time.

Helm, Judy Harris, and Lilian Katz. 2001. *Young Investigators: The Project Approach in the Early Years*. New York: Teachers College Press and Washington, DC: National Association for the Education of Young Children.

This book is divided into chapters that indicate the stages of the Project Approach, explaining what the teacher does and what the children do in each stage. The book concludes with specific examples of projects.

Helm, Judy Harris, Sallee Beneke, and Kathy Steinheimer. 1997. *Windows on Learning: Documenting Young Children's Work*. New York: Teachers College Press.

The primary focus for this book is to guide early childhood educators in using different methods of assessment to document young children's behaviors and progress in acquiring and applying knowledge and skills. There is some discussion of projects, but in the context of how to evaluate what children do in project work and how they go about doing it.

Katz, Lilian, and Sylvia C. Chard. 2000. *Engaging Children's Minds: The Project Approach*. 2d ed. Stamford, CT: Ablex Publishing Co.

Engaging Children's Minds, originally published in 1989, reintroduced the concept of using projects with young children. Prior to this book—and the recent interest in the schools of Reggio Emilia in Italy—virtually no one had written about projects since Kilpatrick and Dewey. In this book, Katz and Chard provide extensive theoretical support for using the Project Approach with young children, ages three–eight. Suggesting that project topics be directly observable in the children's environment, they organize the work of projects into three stages: getting started, field work, and culminating and debriefing events. Their emphasis is on firsthand experiences in researching a topic and having a culminating experience to conclude the project. In implementing the Project Approach, they suggest several topics: the school bus, construction sites, going shopping, shade and shadow studies, hospitals, and so on.

Levy, Steven. 1996. *Starting from Scratch: One Classroom Builds Its Own Curriculum*. Portsmouth, NH: Heinemann.

Clearly written from the perspective of a critical pedagogist, Levy explains his journey as an educator, from summer boys' camp to the constructivist elementary school teacher he is today. His narrative writing style brings readers into his fourth-grade classroom to view the way he develops a sense of community among his students and how that community pursues research to answer important questions.

Wolk, Steven. 1998. *A Democratic Classroom*. Portsmouth, NH: Heinemann.

Relying on his background as a teacher of third- through eighth-grade students, Wolk offers compelling arguments for reconsidering education as it is currently conducted in most American classrooms. He challenges the reader to reinvent teaching, thus reinventing schools. As part of his recommendations about making school more relevant, he devotes an entire chapter to student-selected projects.

Young, Katherine A. 1994. *Constructing Buildings, Bridges and Minds: Building an Integrated Curriculum Through Social Studies*. Portsmouth, NH: Heinemann.

While the teaching method for fifth- and sixth-grade students described in this book is called the project method, it is more like a thematic investigation. The author outlines two projects—the Washington, DC project and the Latin America project. In this approach, the teacher predetermines the final product (constructing replicas) and makes most of the decisions about the learning.

Appendix C

Possible End Products

Museum Exhibits

Museum exhibits are limited only by space and imagination. Exhibits can be set up in a spare classroom (or other unused area—a basement, stage, foyer, nook, etc.) with book reports, artwork, and informative posters on the walls (or bulletin boards). Tables arranged in the middle of the area hold specimens, informative signage, interactive displays, and hands-on experiments. Other areas of the room display facts about the subject, documentation of how the work was done, library of resources, etc.

Hallway Displays

Similar to a museum exhibit but smaller in scope, hallway exhibits utilize the wall space more than table-top displays. Factual information about the subject can be displayed on large pieces of construction paper mounted on the wall or placed on existing bulletin boards. Narrow tables can hold specimens while other information might be hung from the ceiling.

"Living" History Exhibits

These exhibits can be done in groups or by individuals. A group of children might perform a tableau about the subject studied or individual children might dress as a character and present information about his or her subject. They can be as simple as a child standing by a triptych that displays information or as elaborate as the imagination allows, with sets, backdrops, costumes, etc.

Books

A variety of types of books can display knowledge learned in a project. Each child in the class can contribute a page to the book or individual children can each create a book. These can be placed in the school's library, given to a local child care center or senior citizens center, or to another class.

School Newspaper

School newspapers can provide information to a large number of people at one time. A number of computer software programs are available to create newspapers. A "special edition" can celebrate a special or particularly newsworthy event. Quarterly newspapers can become an ongoing project.

Newsletters

As a smaller version of a newspaper, newsletters can be produced in several styles, for example, flyers, informative sheets, or class announcements. Newsletters can be distributed to everyone in the school or to smaller, targeted audiences (perhaps to the neighbors of the school) explaining something the school is doing or to inform people who are at-risk for something, such as informing about smoke alarms and fire safety.

Brochures

Brochures are versatile end products. Competent models are available almost anywhere—at the grocery store or neighborhood businesses. Children can create mock-ups of their brochure by hand or by using computers. Brochures can inform (a class brochure can explain about the class to visitors) or guide (a brochure can describe local museums to newcomers to town).

Videos

Informational videos can be recorded by the children or with adults' help. Videos can be as simple as having the children stand in front of the camera and read their script or can include adding costumes, backdrops, memorized lines, and editing the tape. Copies can be made for distribution or the video can be "looped" to play over and over for a particular audience.

Photo Essays

A display of photographs can document learning. These can stand alone or be a part of a more elaborate presentation. Children can take the photographs, write captions, and design the display.

Manuals

Manuals can be created to teach someone else how to do something the class has learned—how to care for a class pet, plant, younger sibling, etc. Competent models are easily available.

Catalogs

Catalogs can include an illustration and description of something or be more like an annotated bibliography. Because they can be easily photocopied and distributed, they are good for informing a group of people about something.

Field Guides

When used in conjunction with a garden or other outdoor space, a field guide can inform about vegetables, herbs, plants, trees, birds, insects, wildflowers, etc. Photographs or detailed sketches and short informational paragraphs can teach an audience about the topic. Competent models are available from many book publishers.

Games

Children might invent games to illustrate a math or science concept. These are often modeled after familiar board games, like Candyland® or Chutes and Ladders®. The games can be shared with another classroom or with younger children.

Posters

Posters can display children's learning about any topic. They can be placed anywhere in the school and be as elaborate as desired. Common features include using various sizes of print (for title and text), a border, and related illustrations.

Reviews

Reviews can be posted in the school's library to inform other students or parents about characteristics of specific books or genres. Competent models are found in magazines that specialize in reviewing children's literature, such as *The Horn Book*, or online at websites that sell books, such as Amazon.com. Reviews can be compiled into a magazine-style book, placed on large index cards and placed near the card catalogue, or posted in a prominent place for all to see.

Appendix D

Suggested Topics and Research Sources for Applied Learning Projects

These topics and research sources cover a wide range of information. For first projects, we recommend starting small with something familiar to the children. Good first projects include those relating to the classroom environment (pets, flower bed outside the window, etc.) or a need in their school environment (informing others about staff members, school history, etc.). These topics and research sources relate closely to the end products (described in Appendix C).

High Interest Topics	Sources for Research
Their school	Interviews with teachers, staff, students; newsletters from previous years; photograph archive
Their class	Interviews with teacher, administration, families, classmates
Classroom pet	Books, brochures; observation; interviews with pet store owners, students who own the same kind of animal; field trip to pet store
Favorite author	Book catalogs; trade books; interviews with librarians, teachers, and other readers of the author
Growing things	Trade books; instructional books; seed catalogs; interviews with staff at a nursery, parents, or grandparents who garden; field trip to nursery and/or vegetable garden

High Interest Topics	Sources for Research
Hurricanes, tornadoes, and other natural disasters	Books; videotapes; magazine and newspaper articles; interviews with people who have witnessed the natural disaster
Weather	Observation; books; newscasts; meteorologist; Internet sites
Wild animals of all types—birds, mammals, reptiles, amphibians, fish, insects	Observation; books; magazines; biologists; high school or college biology instructors; Internet sites; videotapes
Habitats	Books; magazines; field trips (if possible, even to simulated environments); people who have visited that habitat; videotapes; Internet sites
Historical figures	Books; articles; historians; high school or college history instructors; Internet sites
Countries/cultures	Books; magazines; artifacts; videotapes; language tapes; people who have spent significant time in the country or culture being studied
Games, games played by families	Commercially produced board games; games played by different cultures
Newspapers	Books; newspapers; journalists; columnists; editors
Businesses	Observation; books; interviews with shopkeepers, managers, buyers, and accountants

Appendix E
Involving Families

We believe that everyone benefits when children's families are actively involved in the classroom. We plan different ways to keep families informed and offer them different ways to be involved.

Weekly Letters

Weekly letters summarize the preceding week's events and outline upcoming plans. They include specific books read aloud, directions for games played in the classroom, or homework hints. Reminders of upcoming events, schoolwide projects, or volunteer opportunities are also included.

Articles from Magazines and Professional Journals

Short articles that discuss best practices, explain child development issues or provide practical parenting ideas support parents as they grapple with raising their children. You are also modeling good literacy practices by providing articles for them to read.

Suggested Activities to Extend Classroom Experiences

We suggest age-appropriate activities that families can do together. These usually relate to class activities. Sometimes they relate directly to the classroom learning (like rules for a math game the children are playing in class) or can be a suggestion for a family activity (observe how many cars pass by your house in fifteen minutes and graph the cars' colors or count the windows and doors that are in your house).

Displays of Children's Work

Displays of children's work samples with written descriptions of the purpose of the activity and the learning embedded in the activity show the "how" and the "why" of what is done in school. Photographs expand and clarify the family's understanding of the children's work. Families can see what the class does as a whole and evaluate their child's work individually.

Informal Two-Way Communication

Making it convenient for individual parents to ask questions or make comments encourages this informal two-way communication. We simply provide several sheets of notebook paper stapled into a pocket folder so that parents can write their questions or comments and we can respond on the same page.

Phone Calls

We encourage the families to call us and we call families for informal chats. Sometimes we just share a funny thing a child said or tell an especially nice thing that a child did.

Informal Conversations

We encourage parents to come into the classroom when they can. Drop-ins are welcome as well as scheduled visits. We make our schedule available so parents can join us for a read-aloud or come a few minutes before pickup time to share in our end-of-day class meeting. As parents bring their children to school in the morning, they are encouraged to stay for a while, grab a book, and join the children who are reading.

Conferences

Face-to-face meetings between teacher and families give us opportunities to share stories about their child while interpreting and explaining their child's work. These can be on a scheduled basis or an as-needed basis. Parents sometimes request a conference or we do too.

Monthly Family Meetings

Periodic family gatherings offer a forum for socializing, formal agenda items, and informal discussion about issues that affect the class. This is a good chance for collaborative planning ("Who can help take dictation next week?") and to get class-room volunteers. We try to provide child care for the children so all parents have an opportunity to attend.

Family Field Trips

Inexpensive evening or weekend field trips involve entire families in group activities. We have gone to our local zoo, a grassy field to catch insects, and a hill near a local river to search for fossils. Ideas for family field trips come from the class's activities or the families themselves. Often their connections provide a rich learning experience for the class.

Specific Volunteer Opportunities

At the first of the year, we provide a generic volunteer form for families to complete. This helps us learn about the families' expertise or interests. We ask for general volunteer requests during family meetings and make requests of individual parents. We always follow up after asking for volunteers, encouraging the adults to participate.

Family Nights

These differ from family meetings in that they are an opportunity for families to gather with their children at school to share a class accomplishment, watch a class play, play the children's invented games, or view a child-produced video or museum opening. Family Nights can also be schoolwide learning opportunities, such as Family Math Night with children teaching their parents math games or Family Art Night with teachers and children teaching the families different art techniques.

Appendix F

Learning Embedded in One Project

Knowledge and Skills Embedded in the Rocks and Fossils Exhibit Project

Processes used throughout the project:
- Planning and working as a team member
- Working independently
- Using multiple resources
- Helping others find resources
- Setting work priorities
- Allocating time
- Brainstorming ideas and options
- Negotiating solutions and decisions

Class planning meetings:
- Dictating lists of things to do
- Making group decisions about priorities
- Determining committees to be responsible for portions of the exhibit
- Volunteering for committee work

Research about rocks and fossils:
- Learning information from videos, books, people, field trips
- Asking older students to read expository text
- Writing fact cards about rocks and fossils
- Comparing illustrations and photographs found in books and magazines
- Dictating questions prompted from read-alouds
- Interviewing people about rocks and fossils
- Writing letters to experts to ask questions

- Dictating facts learned from videos, books, and experts
- Counting "facts" and comparing quantities

Field trips to museum and geology department of a university:
- Writing letter to museum personnel and geology professor
- Writing reminders to parents
- Charting names of parents who volunteer to drive for each field trip
- Dividing class into field trip cars
- Sketching exhibits and rocks (including meteorites) from observation
- Taking notes about label copy
- Writing thank you notes to experts at zoo and university

Signage for the exhibit:
- Selecting color scheme for museum
- Deciding how to organize the museum
- Deciding what signs to make
- Die-cutting letters and attaching letters to posterboard

Drawings of "great" pictures:
- Describing details orally and using details in drawings
- Revising drawings to include more details
- Using class-generated criteria for judging individual work

Photo essay:
- Deciding which photographs should be taken to chronicle project
- Taking photographs
- Drafting label copy
- Typing label copy
- Mounting photographs and label copy

Hanging items in museum:
- Sorting facts by source
- Evaluating the exhibit to determine if it shows what has been learned

Borrowing artifacts:
- Writing letters to request borrowing artifacts
- Labeling artifacts
- Returning borrowed artifacts with thank you notes

Creating exhibit brochure:
- Examining brochures to determine components
- Working in small groups to develop different parts of the exhibit brochure
- Drafting, peer response, editing, revising brochure

- Typing brochure copy
- Using reducing function of copier
- Cutting and pasting for layout
- Counting and adding groups to determine number of brochures needed
- Folding brochures

Invitation to families and friends of the class:
- Working in committees
- Collaborating with older students
- Drafting invitation copy
- Typing invitation copy
- Using reducing function of copier
- Cutting and pasting for layout
- Counting and adding groups to determine number of invitations needed
- Folding invitations
- Using telephone book to find addresses
- Addressing envelopes with correct format
- Mailing invitations
- Making phone calls to follow up on requests to reschedule

Planning menu for exhibit opening:
- Setting criteria for food
- Dictating suggested menu
- Comparing suggestions to criteria
- Solving problem of too many drink suggestions
- Voting, comparing quantities, and determining final menu
- Predicting how many guests will be at opening
- Determining appropriate amounts of each menu item

Letters to families about bringing food for the exhibit opening:
- Using invented spelling to convey meaning
- Consulting teacher-transcribed list as resource for spelling words
- Practicing the format of a letter: date, salutation, body, closing
- Using calendar as resource for date
- Doing peer response

Letters to teachers inviting them to the exhibit:
- Work in small groups to draft invitations
- Typing final copy
- Asking adults for response to the draft
- Listing all classes in the school
- Distributing the letter

Advertising posters:
- Using conventional spelling
- Arranging poster in an aesthetic way

Scheduling exhibit tours:
- Responding to requests for tours
- Ensuring that no classes are "double booked"
- Listing all teachers
- Following up with teachers who had not made a reservation

Giving exhibit tours:
- Keeping track of scheduled tours
- Keeping track of time
- Sharing orally what the students learned about rocks and fossils and creating a museum exhibit
- Fielding questions from other students
- Writing answers to written questions submitted to the class

Self-evaluation:
- Dictating what they had done to help create the museum
- Choosing their best work and providing a rationale for that decision

State Reading, Writing, and Math Standards (California, Texas, and Virginia) Met by the Rocks and Fossils Exhibit Project

Reading

During the daily read-aloud and the small-group instruction, the teacher introduced and reinforced skills related to phonemic and phonological awareness, decoding and word recognition, vocabulary and concept development, structural features of informational materials, and comprehension and analysis of grade-level-appropriate texts. In these planned and impromptu lessons, the teacher covered all reading standards mandated for kindergartners in California (California Department of Education 1998) except those related to concepts about print—not included because these students had already learned these concepts—and literary response and analysis—because the focus of the project was on expository text, and reading response was done during other times of the school day. In the same lessons, Virginia's teachers would cover twenty-one of twenty-three of the Standards of Learning (SOL) related to reading, with the two missing SOLs requiring students to identify characters and setting and retell stories. Again, these skills were covered outside project time when the children were involved in shared and guided reading activities. In Texas, teachers involved in this project would cover sixty of the seventy Texas Essential Knowledge and Skills (TEKS, Texas Education Agency 1998) required in the reading standards.

Writing

Within the Rocks and Fossils Exhibit project, the teacher addressed all thirty of the TEKS required in Texas for kindergarten students in the area of writing (Texas Education Agency 1998). If these children had been working in other states, their work would easily have met the standards in those states as well. Students addressed all of the thirteen writing standards required of kindergartners in the state of California (California Department of Education 1998) and eleven of the twelve writing standards required of kindergartners in Virginia (Virginia Board of Education 1995).

Math

Considering the mathematical activities common to most Applied Learning projects, students typically meet one-third to one-half of math standards. Five- and six-year-olds in Virginia would demonstrate their understanding of seven of twenty-one math SOLs. In California, students would meet seventeen of the twenty-two mathematical content standards, and in Texas, students would meet eighteen of thirty-one math TEKS. However, in the Math Games project for second-grade students mentioned in Chapter 4, many more math standards were addressed: twenty of twenty-six SOLs in Virginia, thirty of thirty-six content standards in California, and twenty-six of thirty-four TEKS in Texas.

References

Aliki. 1990. *Fossils Tell of Long Ago*. New York: HarperTrophy.

American Association for the Advancement of Science, Project 2061. 1993. *Benchmarks for Science Literacy*. New York: Oxford University Press.

Baylor, Byrd. 1974. *Everybody Needs a Rock*. Glenview, IL: Scott Foresman.

Bickart, Toni S., Judy Jablon, and Diane Trister Dodge. 1999. *Building the Primary Classroom: A Complete Guide to Teaching and Learning*. Washington, DC: Teaching Strategies and Portsmouth, NH: Heinemann.

Bodrova, Eleana, and Deborah Leong. 1996. *Tools of the Mind: The Vygotsky Approach to Early Childhood Education*. Englewood Cliffs, NJ: Prentice-Hall.

Borgia, Eileen. 1996. "Learning Through Projects." *Scholastic Early Childhood Today* 106: 22–29.

Bredekamp, Sue, and Carol Copple. 1997. *Developmentally Appropriate Practice in Early Childhood Programs*. Rev. ed. Washington, DC: National Association for the Education of Young Children.

Bredekamp, Sue, and Teresa Rosegrant, eds. 1992. *Reaching Potentials: Appropriate Curriculum and Assessment for Young Children*. Vol. 1. Washington, DC: National Association for the Education of Young Children.

———. 1995. *Reaching Potentials: Transforming Early Childhood Curriculum and Assessment*. Vol. 2. Washington, DC: National Association for the Education of Young Children.

Bromley, Karen, Linda Irwin-DeVitis, and Marcia Modlo. 1995. *Graphic Organizers: Visual Strategies for Active Learning*. New York: Scholastic Professional Books.

Bryan, John W. 1999. "Readers' Workshop in a Kindergarten Classroom." *The Reading Teacher* 52 (5): 538–41.

Cameron, Caren, Betty Tate, Daphne MacNaughton, and Colleen Politano. 1997. *Recognition Without Rewards*. Winnipeg, Canada: Peguis Publishers.

Cannon, Janell. 1993. *Stellaluna*. New York: Scholastic.

Chard, Sylvia. 1998a. *The Project Approach: Making Curriculum Come Alive (Book 1)*. New York: Scholastic.

———. 1998b. *The Project Approach: Managing Successful Projects (Book 2)*. New York: Scholastic.

Cherry, Lynne. 1990. *The Great Kapok Tree*. New York: Harcourt.

Clements, D. 1998. Young children and technology. ERIC Document Reproduction Services No. 416 991.

Cooke, F. J. 1926. "Fundamental Considerations Underlying the Curriculum of the Francis W. Parker School." In *The Twenty-Sixth Yearbook of the NSSE: Part I*, edited by G. M. Whipple, 305–13. Bloomington, IL: Public School Publishing.

Davis, B. C., and Daniel D. Shade. 1994. Integrate, don't isolate!—Computers in the early childhood curriculum. ERIC Document Reproduction Services No. 376 991.

Denton, Paula, and Roxann Kriete. 2000. *The First Six Weeks of School*. Greenfield, MA: Northeast Foundation for Children.

dePaola, Tomie. 1988. *Strega Nona*. New York: Aladdin Paperbacks.

Developmental Studies Center. 1996. *Ways We Want Our Class to Be: Class Meetings That Build Commitment to Kindness and Learning*. Oakland, CA: Author.

DeVries, Rheta, and Betty Zan. 1994. *Moral Classrooms, Moral Children: Creating a Constructivist Atmosphere in Early Education*. New York: Teachers College Press.

Dewey, John. 1938. *Experience and Education*. New York: Collier Books.

———. 2001. "Project Reptile," *Science and Children* 38 (7): 30–35.

Diffily, Deborah. 1996. "The Project Approach: A Museum Exhibit Created by Kindergartners." *Young Children* 51 (2): 72–75.

Diffily, Deborah, and Pamela O. Fleege. 1993. "The Power of Portfolios for Communicating with Families." *Dimensions of Early Childhood* 22 (2): 40–41.

Edwards, Carolyn, Lella Gandini, and George Forman, eds. 1998. *The Hundred Languages of Children: The Reggio Emilia Approach–Advanced Reflections*. 2d ed. Greenwich, CT: Ablex.

Elkind, David. 1998. Educating young children in math, science, and technology. ERIC Document Reproduction Services No. 416 993.

Farr, Roger C., and Bruce Tone. 1994. *Portfolio and Performance Assessment: Helping Students Evaluate Their Progress as Readers and Writers*. Fort Worth, TX: Harcourt Brace.

Fisher, Bobbi. 1998. *Joyful Learning in Kindergarten*. Portsmouth, NH: Heinemann.

Flagg, Ann. 1998. *Rubrics, Checklists & Other Assessments for the Science You Teach*. New York: Scholastic Professional Books.

Fountas, Irene C., and Gay Su Pinnell. 1996. *Guided Reading: Good First Teaching for All Children*. Portsmouth, NH: Heinemann.

Gardner, Howard. 1983. *Frames of Mind: The Theory of Multiple Intelligences*. New York: Basic Books.

———. 1993. *Multiple Intelligences: The Theory in Practice*. New York: Basic Books.

———. 1998. *Building on Children's Strengths: The Experience of Project Spectrum (Project Zero Frameworks for Early Childhood Education)*. Vol. 1. New York: Teachers College Press.

Gemmett, R. 1977. A monograph on interpersonal communication. ERIC Document Reproduction Services Number ED 153 323.

Glazer, Susan Mandel. 1999. "Using *KWL* Folders." *Teaching PreK–8 29* (4): 106–108.

Goodrich, Heidi. 1996/97. "Understanding Rubrics." *Educational Leadership 54* (4): 14–18.

Gorham, Peter J., and Pamela Nason. 1997. "Why Make Teachers' Work More Visible to Parents?" *Young Children 52* (5): 22–26.

Grace, Cathy, and Elizabeth F. Shores. 1991. *The Portfolio and Its Use: Developmentally Appropriate Assessment of Young Children*. Little Rock, AR: Southern Early Childhood Association.

Hartman, Jeanette A., and Carolyn Eckerty. 1995. "Projects in the Early Years." *Childhood Education 71* (3): 141–49.

Harwayne, Shelley. 2000. *Lifetime Guarantees: Toward Ambitious Literacy Teaching*. Portsmouth, NH: Heinemann.

Healy, Jane M. 1998. *Failure to Connect: How Computers Affect Our Children's Minds— For Better and Worse*. New York: Simon and Schuster.

Helm, Judy Harris, Sallee Beneke, and Kathy Steinheimer. 1997. *Windows on Learning: Documenting Young Children's Work*. New York: Teachers College Press.

Helm, Judy Harris, and Lilian Katz. 2001. *Young Investigators: The Project Approach in the Early Years*. New York: Teachers College Press and Washington, DC: National Association for the Education of Young Children.

Hindley, Joanne. 1996. *In the Company of Children*. Portland, ME: Stenhouse.

Katz, Lilian. 1996. "Lilian Katz on the Project Approach." *Scholastic Early Childhood Today 106*: 20–21.

Katz, Lilian, and Sylvia Chard. 2000. *Engaging Children's Minds: The Project Approach*. 2d ed. Stamford, CT: Ablex.

Katz, Lilian G., and Diane McClellan. 1997. *Fostering Children's Social Competence: The Teacher's Role*. Washington, DC: National Association for the Education of Young Children.

Kirkpatrick, William H. 1918. "The Project Method," *Teachers College Record 19*(4): 319–35.

Kohn, Alfie. 1996. *Beyond Discipline: From Compliance to Community*. Alexandria, VA: Association for Supervision and Curriculum Development.

Lantieri, Linda, and Janet Patti. 1996. *Waging Peace in Our Schools.* Boston: Beacon Press.

Levy, Steven. 1996. *Starting from Scratch: One Classroom Builds Its Own Curriculum.* Portsmouth, NH: Heinemann.

Lewin, Larry, and Betty Jane Shoemaker. 1998. *Great Performances: Creating Classroom-Based Assessment Tasks.* Alexandria, VA: Association for Supervision and Curriculum Development.

Lindquist, Tarry. 1995. *Seeing the Whole Through Social Studies.* Portsmouth, NH: Heinemann.

Manning, Maryann, Gary Manning, and Roberta Long. 1997. *Theme Immersion Compendium for Social Studies Teaching.* Portsmouth, NH: Heinemann.

McCarrier, Andrea, Gay Su Pinnell, and Irene Fountas. 1999. *Interactive Writing: How Language and Literacy Come Together, K–2.* Portsmouth, NH: Heinemann.

Mitchell, Lucy Sprague. 1934/1971. *Young Geographers: How They Explore the World and How They Map the World.* New York: Bank Street.

National Center on Education and the Economy. 1997. *Performance Standards.* Vol. 1, *Elementary School.* Washington, DC: Author.

National Council for Teachers of English/International Reading Association. 1996. *Standards for the English Language Arts.* Urbana, IL: Authors.

National Council of Teachers of Mathematics. 2000. *Principles and Assessment for School Mathematics.* Reston, VA: Author.

National Research Council. 1995. *National Science Education Standards.* Washington, DC: National Academy Press.

Nelsen, Jane, and H. Stephen Glenn. 1996. *Positive Discipline.* New York: Ballentine Books.

Neuman, Susan B., Carol Copple, and Sue Bredekamp. 2000. *Learning to Read and Write: Developmentally Appropriate Practices for Young Children.* Washington, DC: National Association for the Education of Young Children.

Oates, Joyce Carol. 1997. "The Practice of Writing: The Writing Workshop." *Writer 110* (10): 7–11.

Ogle, Donna. 1986. "K-W-L: A Teaching Model That Develops Active Reading of Expository Text." *The Reading Teacher* 39: 564–70.

Pallotta, Jerry. 1989. *The Yucky Reptile Alphabet Book.* Watertown, MA: Charlesbridge Publishing.

Parker, Ruth E., and Kathy Richardson. 1993. *Mathematical Power: Lessons from a Classroom.* Portsmouth, NH: Heinemann.

Paulson, F. Leon, Pearl R. Paulson, and C. A. Meyer. 1991. "What Makes a Portfolio a Portfolio?" *Educational Leadership* 48 (5): 60–64.

Perrone, Vito, ed. 1991. *Expanding Student Assessment*. Alexandria, VA: Association for Supervision and Curriculum Development.

Peters, Dorothy. 2000. *Taking Cues from Kids*. Portsmouth, NH: Heinemann.

Piaget, Jean. 1936/1952. *The Origins of Intelligence in Children*. Translated by M. Cook. New York: Norton.

Pratt, Caroline. 1926. "Curriculum-Making in the City and Country School." In *The Twenty-Sixth Yearbook of the NSSE: Part I*, edited by G. M. Whipple, 327–32. Bloomington, IL: Public School Publishing.

Puckett, Margaret B., and Janet K. Black. 2000. *Authentic Assessment of the Young Child: Celebrating Development and Learning*. 2d ed. Columbus, OH: Merrill/Prentice-Hall.

Puckett, Margaret B., and Deborah Diffily. 1999. *Teaching Young Children: An Introduction to the Early Childhood Profession*. Fort Worth, TX: Harcourt Brace.

Rankin, Baji. 1998. "Curriculum Development in Reggio Emilia: A Long Term Curriculum Project About Dinosaurs." In *The Hundred Languages of Children*, edited by Carolyn Edwards, Lella Gandini, and George Forman, 215–37. Norwood, NJ: Ablex.

Rich, Dorothy. 1997. *MegaSkills: Building Children's Achievement for the Information Age*. New York: Houghton Mifflin.

Routman, Regie. 1996. *Literacy at the Crossroads*. Portsmouth, NH: Heinemann.

Saul, Wendy, Jeanne Reardon, Anne Schmidt, Charles Pearce, Dana Blackwood, and Mary Dickinson Bird. 1993. *Science Workshop: A Whole Language Approach*. Portsmouth, NH: Heinemann.

Schaps, Eric. 1998. "Risks and Rewards of Community Building." *Thrust for Educational Leadership 28* (1): 6–10.

Schneider, Evelyn. 1996. "Giving Students a Voice in the Classroom." *Educational Leadership 54* (1): 22–27.

Tanner, Laurel N. 1997. *Dewey's Laboratory School: Lessons for Today*. New York: Teachers College Press.

Teale, William. H. 1995. "Young Children and Reading: Trends Across the Twentieth Century." *Journal of Education 177* (3): 95–128.

Texas Education Agency. 1998. *Texas Essential Knowledge and Skills*. Austin, TX: Author.

Tombari, Martin, and Gary Borich. 1999. *Authentic Assessment in the Classroom: Applications and Practice*. Upper Saddle River, NJ: Merrill.

Tomlinson, Carol Ann. 1999. *The Differentiated Classroom: Responding to the Needs of All Learners*. Alexandria, VA: Association for Supervision and Curriculum Development.

Trepanier-Street, Mary. 1993. "What's So New About the Project Approach?" *Childhood Education 70* (1): 25–28.

U.S. Department of Labor. 1991. *What Work Requires of Schools: A SCANS Report for America 2000*. Washington, DC: U. S. Government Printing Office.

———. 1992. *SCANS in the Schools*. Washington, DC: U. S. Government Printing Office.

Vygotsky, Lev Semenovich. 1934/1986. *Thought and Language*. Cambridge, MA: MIT Press.

Ward, Geoff. 1988. *I've Got a Project on. . . .* Rozelle, Australia: Primary English Teaching Association.

Wolk, Steven. 1998. *A Democratic Classroom*. Portsmouth, NH: Heinemann.

Young, Katherine A. 1994. *Constructing Buildings, Bridges and Minds: Building an Integrated Curriculum Through Social Studies*. Portsmouth, NH: Heinemann.

Zemelman, Steven, Harvey Daniels, and Arthur A. Hyde. 1998. *Best Practice: New Standards for Teaching and Learning in America's Schools*, 2nd ed. Portsmouth, NH: Heinemann.

Zinsser, William K. 1998. *On Writing Well: The Classic Guide to Writing Nonfiction*. New York: Harper.